Afghanistan
a country study

Federal Research Division
Library of Congress

Foreword

This volume is one in a continuing series of books prepared by the Federal Research Division of the Library of Congress under the Country Studies/Area Handbook Program sponsored by the Department of the Army. The last two pages of this book list the other published studies.

Most books in the series deal with a particular foreign country, describing and analyzing its political, economic, social, and national security systems and institutions, and examining the interrelationships of those systems and the ways they are shaped by historical and cultural factors. Each study is written by a multidisciplinary team of social scientists. The authors seek to provide a basic understanding of the observed society, striving for a dynamic rather than a static portrayal. Particular attention is devoted to the people who make up the society, their origins, dominant beliefs and values, their common interests and the issues on which they are divided, the nature and extent of their involvement with national institutions, and their attitudes toward each other and toward their social system and political order.

The books represent the analysis of the authors and should not be construed as an expression of an official United States government position, policy, or decision. The authors have sought to adhere to accepted standards of scholarly objectivity. Corrections, additions, and suggestions for changes from readers will be welcomed for use in future editions.

Louis R. Mortimer
Chief
Federal Research Division
Library of Congress
Washington, DC 20540-4840

AFGHANISTAN: BACKGROUND NOTES

U.S. DEPARTMENT OF STATE

Bureau of South Asian Affairs
October 2001

Table of Contents

People XV

History XV

Government XXIV

Political Conditions XXIV

Economy XXV

Foreign Relations XXIX

U.S. Relations XXXIII

Travel/Business XXXV

PROFILE

OFFICIAL NAME:

Islamic State of Afghanistan
(The Taliban regime refers to the country as the Islamic Emirate of
Afghanistan.)

Geography

Area: 648,000 sq. km. (252,000 sq. mi.); slightly smaller than Texas.
Cities: *Capital* (1999/2000 UN est.) Kabul--1,780,000. *Other cities*
(1988 UN est.; current figures are probably significantly higher)--
Kandahar (226,000); Herat (177,000); Mazar-e-Sharif (131,000);
Jalalabad (58,000); Konduz (57,000).
Terrain: Landlocked; mostly mountains and desert.
Climate: Dry, with cold winters and hot summers.

People

Nationality: *Noun and adjective*--Afghan(s).
Population (July 2000 est.): 25,853,797. More than 4 million Afghans
live outside the country, mainly in Pakistan and Iran.
Annual population growth rate (2000 est.): 3.54%. (**Note:** This rate
reflected return of refugees from Iran and is probably much reduced.)
Main ethnic groups: Pashtun, Tajik, Hazara, Uzbek, Turkmen,
Aimaq, Baluch, Nuristani, Kizilbash.
Religions: Sunni Muslim 84%, Shi'a Muslim 15%, other 1%.
Main languages: Dari (Afghan Persian), Pashto.
Education: Only a small percentage of children attend school.
Literacy (1999 est.)--31.5% (male: 47.2%, female: 15 %), but real
figures may be lower given breakdown of education system and flight
of educated Afghans.
Health: *Infant mortality rate* (2000)--149.28 /1,000. *Life expectancy*
(2000 est.)--46.62 yrs. (male); 45.1 yrs. (female).
Work force: Mostly in rural agriculture; number cannot be estimated
due to conflict.

Government

Type: Afghanistan identifies itself as an "Islamic state."
Independence: August 19, 1919 (from U.K. control over Afghan foreign affairs).
Organization: There is no functioning central government. The country is divided among fighting factions. The UN recognizes the Islamic State of Afghanistan headed by Burhanuddin Rabbani, which controls about 10% of the country as of October 2001. The Taliban, a radical Islamic movement, occupies about 90% of the country. Its supreme head is Mullah Omar.
Flag: Adopted in 1992, the flag has three horizontal bands--green, white, and black--with the great seal of Afghanistan superimposed on the bands. The Taliban uses a plain white flag.

Economy

GDP: $3 billion (1991 est.) and may well be correct. Purchasing parity power (1999 est.) was $21 billion.
Natural resources: Natural gas, oil, coal, copper, chromite, talc, barites, sulfur, lead, zinc, iron, salt, precious and semiprecious stones.
Agriculture (at least 65% of GDP): *Products*--wheat, corn, barley, rice, cotton, fruit, nuts, karakul pelts, wool, and mutton.
Industry (estimated 20% of GDP): *Types*--smallscale production for domestic use of textiles, soap, furniture, shoes, fertilizer, and cement; hand-woven carpets for export; natural gas, precious and semiprecious gemstones.
Trade (1996 est.): *Exports*--$80 million (does not include opium): opium, fruits and nuts, hand-woven carpets, wool, cotton, hides and pelts, precious and semiprecious gems. *Major markets*--Central Asian Republics, Pakistan, Iran, EC, India. Estimates show that the figure for 2001 is much reduced, except for opium. *Imports*--$150 million (1996 est.): food, petroleum products, and consumer goods. Estimates show that imports have been severely reduced in 2001. *Major suppliers*--Central Asian Republics, Pakistan, Iran.
Currency: The Northern Alliance and the Taliban maintain separate currencies though both are called the afghani. Both are highly inflated

with rates fluctuating frequently. The market rate during much of 2001 for each currency exceeded 50,000 Afghanis=U.S.$1. The Pakistani rupee and other foreign currencies are frequently used as legal tender.

PEOPLE

Afghanistan's ethnically and linguistically mixed population reflects its location astride historic trade and invasion routes leading from Central Asia into South and Southwest Asia. Pashtuns are the dominant ethnic group, accounting for about 38% of the population. Tajik (25%), Hazara (19%), Uzbek (6%), Aimaq, Turkmen, Baluch and other small groups also are represented. Dari (Afghan Persian) and Pashto are official languages. Dari is spoken by more than one-third of the population as a first language and serves as a lingua franca for most Afghans, though the Taliban use Pashto. Tajik, Uzbek, and Turkmen are spoken widely in the north. Smaller groups throughout the country also speak more than 70 other languages and numerous dialects.

Afghanistan is an Islamic country. An estimated 84% of the population is Sunni, following the Hanafi school of jurisprudence; the remainder is predominantly Shi'a, mainly Hazara. Despite attempts during the years of communist rule to secularize Afghan society, Islamic practices pervade all aspects of life. In fact, Islam served as the principal basis for expressing opposition to the communists and the Soviet invasion. Likewise, Islamic religious tradition and codes, together with traditional practices, provide the principal means of controlling personal conduct and settling legal disputes. Excluding urban populations in the principal cities, most Afghans are divided into tribal and other kinship-based groups, which follow traditional customs and religious practices.

HISTORY

Afghanistan, often called the crossroads of Central Asia, has had a turbulent history. In 328 BC, Alexander the Great entered the territory of present-day Afghanistan, then part of the Persian Empire, to capture Bactria (present-day Balkh). Invasions by the Scythians, White Huns, and Turks followed in succeeding centuries. In AD 642, Arabs invaded the entire region and introduced Islam.

Arab rule quickly gave way to the Persians, who controlled the area until conquered by the Turkic Ghaznavids in 998. Mahmud of Ghazni (998-1030) consolidated the conquests of his predecessors and turned Ghazni into a great cultural center as well as a base for frequent forays into India. Following Mahmud's short-lived dynasty, various princes attempted to rule sections of the country until the Mongol invasion of 1219. The Mongol invasion, led by Genghis Khan, resulted in massive slaughter of the population, destruction of many cities, including Herat, Ghazni, and Balkh, and the despoliation of fertile agricultural areas.

Following Genghis Khan's death in 1227, a succession of petty chiefs and princes struggled for supremacy until late in the 14th century, when one of his descendants, Tamerlane, incorporated Afghanistan into his own vast Asian empire. Babur, a descendant of Tamerlane and the founder of India's Moghul dynasty at the beginning of the 16th century, made Kabul the capital of an Afghan principality.

In 1747, Ahmad Shah Durrani, the founder of what is known today as Afghanistan, established his rule. A Pashtun, Durrani was elected king by a tribal council after the assassination of the Persian ruler Nadir Shah at Khabushan in the same year. Throughout his reign, Durrani consolidated chieftainships, petty principalities, and fragmented provinces into one country. His rule extended from Mashad in the west to Kashmir and Delhi in the east, and from the Amu Darya (Oxus) River in the north to the Arabian Sea in the south. With the exception of a 9-month period in 1929, all of Afghanistan's rulers until the 1978 Marxist coup were from Durrani's Pashtun tribal confederation, and all were members of that tribe's Mohammadzai clan after 1818.

European Influence

Collision between the expanding British and Russian Empires

significantly influenced Afghanistan during the 19th century in what was termed "The Great Game." British concern over Russian advances in Central Asia and growing influence in Persia culminated in two Anglo-Afghan wars. The first (1839-42) resulted not only in the destruction of a British army, but is remembered today as an example of the ferocity of Afghan resistance to foreign rule. The second Anglo-Afghan war (1878-80) was sparked by Amir Sher Ali's refusal to accept a British mission in Kabul. This conflict brought Amir Abdur Rahman to the Afghan throne. During his reign (1880-1901), the British and Russians officially established the boundaries of what would become modern Afghanistan. The British retained effective control over Kabul's foreign affairs.

Afghanistan remained neutral during World War I, despite German encouragement of anti-British feelings and Afghan rebellion along the borders of British India. The Afghan king's policy of neutrality was not universally popular within the country, however.

Habibullah, Abdur Rahman's son and successor, was assassinated in 1919, possibly by family members opposed to British influence. His third son, Amanullah, regained control of Afghanistan's foreign policy after launching the Third Anglo-Afghan war with an attack on India in the same year. During the ensuing conflict, the war-weary British relinquished their control over Afghan foreign affairs by signing the Treaty of Rawalpindi in August 1919. In commemoration of this event, Afghans celebrate August 19 as their Independence Day.

Reform and Reaction

King Amanullah (1919-29) moved to end his country's traditional isolation in the years following the Third Anglo-Afghan war. He established diplomatic relations with most major countries and, following a 1927 tour of Europe and Turkey--during which he noted the modernization and secularization advanced by Ataturk--introduced several reforms intended to modernize Afghanistan. Some of these, such as the abolition of the traditional Muslim veil for women and the opening of a number of co-educational schools, quickly alienated many tribal and religious leaders. Faced with overwhelming armed opposition, Amanullah was forced to abdicate in January 1929 after Kabul fell to forces led by Bacha-i-Saqao, a Tajik brigand. Prince Nadir Khan, a cousin of Amanullah's, in turn defeated Bacha-i-Saqao in October of the same year and, with considerable Pashtun tribal support, was declared King Nadir Shah. Four years later, however, he was assassinated in a revenge killing by a Kabul student.

Mohammad Zahir Shah, Nadir Khan's 19-year-old son, succeeded to the throne and reigned from 1933 to 1973. In 1964, King Zahir Shah promulgated a liberal constitution providing for a two-chamber legislature to which the king appointed one-third of the deputies. The people elected another third, and the remainder were selected indirectly by provincial assemblies. Although Zahir's "experiment in democracy" produced few lasting reforms, it permitted the growth of unofficial extremist parties on both the left and the right. These included the communist People's Democratic Party of Afghanistan (PDPA), which had close ideological ties to the Soviet Union. In 1967, the PDPA split into two major rival factions: the Khalq (Masses) faction headed by Nur Muhammad Taraki and Hafizullah Amin and supported by elements within the military, and the Parcham (Banner) faction led by Babrak Karmal. The split reflected ethnic, class, and ideological divisions within Afghan society.

Zahir's cousin, Sardar Mohammad Daoud, served as his Prime Minister from 1953 to 1963. During his tenure as Prime Minister, Daoud solicited military and economic assistance from both Washington and Moscow and introduced controversial social policies of a reformist nature. Daoud's alleged support for the creation of a Pashtun state in the Pakistan-Afghan border area heightened tensions with Pakistan and eventually resulted in Daoud's dismissal in March 1963.

Daoud's Republic (1973-78) and the April 1978 Coup

Amid charges of corruption and malfeasance against the royal family and poor economic conditions created by the severe 1971-72 drought, former Prime Minister Daoud seized power in a military coup on July 17, 1973. Zahir Shah fled the country eventually finding refuge in Italy. Daoud abolished the monarchy, abrogated the 1964 constitution, and declared Afghanistan a republic with himself as its first President and Prime Minister. His attempts to carry out badly needed economic and social reforms met with little success, and the new constitution promulgated in February 1977 failed to quell chronic political instability.

Seeking to exploit more effectively mounting popular disaffection, the PDPA reunified with Moscow's support. On April 27, 1978, the PDPA initiated a bloody coup, which resulted in the overthrow and murder of Daoud and most of his family. Nur Muhammad Taraki, Secretary General of the PDPA, became President of the Revolutionary Council and Prime Minister of the newly established Democratic Republic of Afghanistan.

Opposition to the Marxist government emerged almost immediately. During its first 18 months of rule, the PDPA brutally imposed a Marxist-style "reform" program, which ran counter to deeply rooted Afghan traditions.

Decrees abolishing usury, forcing changes in marriage customs, and pushing through an ill-conceived land reform were particularly misunderstood virtually all Afghans. In addition, thousands of members of the traditional elite, the religious establishment, and the intelligentsia were imprisoned, tortured, or murdered. Conflicts within the PDPA also surfaced early and resulted in exiles, purges, imprisonments, and executions.

By the summer of 1978, a revolt began in the Nuristan region of eastern Afghanistan and quickly spread into a countrywide insurgency. In September 1979, Hafizullah Amin, who had earlier been Prime Minister and Minister of Defense, seized power from Taraki after a palace shootout. Over the next 2 months, instability plagued Amin's regime as he moved against perceived enemies in the PDPA. By December, party morale was crumbling, and the insurgency was growing.

The Soviet Invasion

The Soviet Union moved quickly to take advantage of the April 1978 coup. In December 1978, Moscow signed a new bilateral treaty of friendship and cooperation with Afghanistan, and the Soviet military assistance program increased significantly. The regime's survival increasingly was dependent upon Soviet military equipment and advisers as the insurgency spread and the Afghan army began to collapse.

By October 1979, however, relations between Afghanistan and the Soviet Union were tense as Hafizullah Amin refused to take Soviet advice on how to stabilize and consolidate his government. Faced with a deteriorating security situation on December 24, 1979, large numbers of Soviet airborne forces, joining thousands of Soviet troops already on the ground, began to land in Kabul under the pretext of a field exercise. On December 26, these invasion forces killed Hafizullah Amin and installed Babrak Karmal, exiled leader of the Parcham faction, bringing him back from Czechoslovakia and making him Prime Minister. Massive Soviet ground forces invaded from the north on December 27.

Following the invasion, the Karmal regime, although backed by an expeditionary force that grew as large as 120,000 Soviet troops, was unable to establish authority outside Kabul. As much as 80% of the countryside, including parts of Herat and Kandahar, eluded effective government control. An overwhelming majority of Afghans opposed the communist regime, either actively or passively. Afghan freedom fighters (mujahidin) made it almost impossible for the regime to maintain a system of local government outside major urban centers. Poorly armed at first, in 1984 the mujahidin began receiving substantial assistance in the form of weapons and training from the U.S. and other outside powers.

In May 1985, the seven principal Peshawar-based guerrilla organizations formed an alliance to coordinate their political and military operations against the Soviet occupation. Late in 1985, the mujahidin were active in and around Kabul, launching rocket attacks and conducting operations against the communist government. The failure of the Soviet Union to win over a significant number of Afghan collaborators or to rebuild a viable Afghan army forced it to bear an increasing responsibility for fighting the resistance and for civilian administration.

Soviet and popular displeasure with the Karmal regime led to its demise in May 1986. Karmal was replaced by Muhammad Najibullah, former chief of the Afghan secret police (KHAD). Najibullah had established a reputation for brutal efficiency during his tenure as KHAD chief. As Prime Minister, Najibullah was ineffective and highly dependent on Soviet support. Undercut by deep-seated divisions within the PDPA, regime efforts to broaden its base of support proved futile.

The Geneva Accords and Their Aftermath

By the mid-1980s, the tenacious Afghan resistance movement--aided by the United States, Saudi Arabia, Pakistan, and others--was exacting a high price from the Soviets, both militarily within Afghanistan and by souring the U.S.S.R.'s relations with much of the Western and Islamic world. Although informal negotiations for a Soviet withdrawal from Afghanistan had been underway since 1982, it was not until 1988 that the Governments of Pakistan and Afghanistan, with the United States and Soviet Union serving as guarantors, signed an agreement settling the major differences between them. The agreement, known as the Geneva accords, included five major documents, which, among other things, called for U.S. and Soviet noninterference in the internal affairs of Pakistan and Afghanistan, the right of refugees to return to Afghanistan without fear of persecution or harassment, and, most importantly, a timetable that ensured full Soviet withdrawal from Afghanistan by February 15, 1989. About 14,500 Soviet and an estimated one million Afghan lives were lost between 1979 and the Soviet withdrawal in 1989.

Significantly, the mujahidin were neither party to the negotiations nor to the 1988 agreement and, consequently, refused to accept the terms of the accords. As a result, the civil war continued after the Soviet withdrawal, which was completed in February 1989. Najibullah's regime, though failing to win popular support, territory, or international recognition, was able to remain in power until 1992 but collapsed after the defection of Gen. Abdul Rashid Dostam and his Uzbek militia in March. However, when the victorious mujahidin entered Kabul to assume control over the city and the central government, a new round of internecine fighting began between the various militias, which had coexisted only uneasily during the Soviet occupation. With the demise of their common enemy, the militias' ethnic, clan, religious, and personality differences surfaced, and the civil war continued.

Seeking to resolve these differences, the leaders of the Peshawar-based mujahidin groups established an interim Islamic Jihad Council in mid-April to assume power in Kabul. Moderate leader Prof. Sibghatullah Mojaddedi was to chair the council for 2 months, after which a 10-member leadership council composed of mujahidin leaders and presided over by the head of the Jamiat-i-Islami, Prof. Burhanuddin Rabbani, was to be set up for 4 months. During this 6-month period, a Loya Jirga, or grand council of Afghan elders and notables, would convene and designate an interim administration which would hold power up to a year, pending elections.

But in May 1992, Rabbani prematurely formed the leadership council, undermining Mojaddedi's fragile authority. In June, Mojaddedi surrendered power to the Leadership Council, which then elected Rabbani as President. Nonetheless, heavy fighting broke out in August 1992 in Kabul between forces loyal to President Rabbani and rival factions, particularly those who supported Gulbuddin Hekmatyar's Hezb-i-Islami. After Rabbani extended his tenure in December 1992, fighting in the capital flared up in January and February 1993. The Islamabad Accord, signed in March 1993, which appointed Hekmatyar as Prime Minister, failed to have a lasting effect. A follow-up agreement, the Jalalabad Accord, called for the militias to be disarmed but was never fully implemented. Through 1993, Hekmatyar's Hezb-i-Islami forces, allied with the Shi'a Hezb-i-Wahdat militia, clashed intermittently with Rabbani and Masood's Jamiat forces. Cooperating with Jamiat were militants of Sayyaf's

Ittehad-i-Islami and, periodically, troops loyal to ethnic Uzbek strongman Abdul Rashid Dostam. On January 1, 1994, Dostam switched sides, precipitating largescale fighting in Kabul and in northern provinces, which caused thousands of civilian casualties in Kabul and elsewhere and created a new wave of displaced persons and refugees. The country sank even further into anarchy, forces loyal to Rabbani and Masood, both ethnic Tajiks, controlled Kabul and much of the northeast, while local warlords exerted power over the rest of the country.

Rise of the Taliban

In reaction to the anarchy and warlordism prevalent in the country, and the lack of Pashtun representation in the Kabul government, a movement of former mujahidin arose. Many Taliban had been educated in madrassas in Pakistan and were largely from rural Pashtun backgrounds. The name "Talib" itself means pupil. This group dedicated itself to removing the warlords, providing order, and imposing Islam on the country. It received considerable support from Pakistan. In 1994 it developed enough strength to capture the city of Kandahar from a local warlord and proceeded to expand its control throughout Afghanistan, occupying Kabul in September 1996. By the end of 1998, the Taliban occupied about 90% of the country, limiting the opposition largely to a small largely Tajik corner in the northeast and the Panjshir valley. Efforts by the UN, prominent Afghans living outside the country, and other interested countries to bring about a peaceful solution to the continuing conflict came to naught, largely because of intransigence on the part of the Taliban.

The Taliban has sought to impose an extreme interpretation of Islam-- based in part upon rural Pashtun tradition--upon the entire country and committed massive human rights violations, particularly directed against women and girls, in the process. Women are restricted from working outside the home, pursuing an education, are not to leave their homes without an accompanying male relative, and forced to wear a traditional body-covering garment called the burka. The

Taliban committed serious atrocities against minority populations, particularly the Shi'a Hazara ethnic group, and killed noncombatants in several well-documented instances. In 2001, as part of a drive against relics of Afghanistan's pre-Islamic past, the Taliban destroyed two large statues of the Buddha outside of the city of Bamiyan and announced destruction of all pre-Islamic statues in Afghanistan, including the remaining holdings of the Kabul Museum.

Since the mid-1990s the Taliban has provided sanctuary to Usama bin Laden, a Saudi national who had fought with them against the Soviets, and provided a base for his and other terrorist organizations. The UN Security Council repeatedly sanctioned the Taliban for these activities. Bin Laden is believed to provide both financial and political support to the Taliban. Bin Laden and his al Qaeda group were charged with the bombing of the U.S. embassies in Nairobi and Dar Es Salaam in 1998, and in August 1998 the United States launched a cruise missile attack against bin Laden's terrorist camp in Afghanistan. Bin Laden and al Qaeda are believed to be responsible for the September 11, 2001 terrorist acts in the United States, among other crimes.

In September, agents working on behalf of the Taliban and believed to be associated with bin Laden's al Qaeda group assassinated Northern Alliance Defense Minister and chief military commander Ahmed Shah Masood, a hero of the Afghan resistance against the Soviets and the Taliban's principal military opponent. Following the Taliban's repeated refusal to expel bin Laden and his group and end its support for international terrorism, the U.S. and its partners in the anti-terrorist coalition began a campaign on October 7, 2001, targeting terrorist facilities and various Taliban military and political assets within Afghanistan.

GOVERNMENT AND POLITICAL CONDITIONS

There is no functioning central government. As of October 2001, the Taliban controlled approximately 90% of the country, including the capital of Kabul, and all major urban areas except Faizabad. A 1997 Taliban edict renamed the country the Islamic Emirate of Afghanistan and installed Taliban leader Mullah Omar as Head of State and "Commander of the Faithful." He held all ultimate authority. The Taliban's power structure has narrowed over time and become increasingly hard-line. Its main, consultative bodies, the shuras, reportedly no longer function.

A rival regime, the Islamic State of Afghanistan (also called the United Front and/or Northern Alliance), nominally headed by Burhanuddin Rabbani, an ethnic Tajik, controlled about 10% of the country, mostly Tajik areas in the extreme northeast. The Rabbani regime controlled most Afghan embassies and retained Afghanistan's seat at the United Nations.

Principal Government Officials

President (Northern Alliance)--Burhanuddin Rabbani
Minister of Foreign Affairs (Northern Alliance)--Dr. Abdullah

Commander of the Faithful (Amir-ul-Momineen) and Head of State (Taliban)-- Mullah Mohammad Omar
Foreign Minister--Wakil Ahmad Mutawakil

The United States suspended operation of the Afghan Embassy in Washington on August 21, 1997. The Northern Alliance maintains a Consulate General in New York City co-located with its UN Mission at 360 Lexington Ave., 11th Fl., New York, NY 10017 (Tel. 212-972-1212).

ECONOMY

Historically, there has been a dearth of information and reliable statistics about Afghanistan's economy. The Soviet invasion and ensuing civil war destroyed much of the underdeveloped country's limited infrastructure and disrupted normal patterns of economic activity. Gross domestic product has fallen substantially over the past 20 years because of loss of labor and capital and disruption of trade and transport. Continuing internal strife hampered both domestic efforts at reconstruction as well as international aid efforts.

Agriculture

The Afghan economy continues to be overwhelmingly agricultural, despite the fact that only 12% of its total land area is arable and less than 6% currently is cultivated. Agricultural production is constrained by an almost total dependence on erratic winter snows and spring rains for water; irrigation is primitive. Relatively little use is made of machines, chemical fertilizer, or pesticides.

Grain production is Afghanistan's traditional agricultural mainstay. Overall agricultural production dramatically declined following 3 years of drought as well as the sustained fighting, instability in rural areas, and deteriorated infrastructure. Soviet efforts to disrupt production in resistance-dominated areas also contributed to this decline as did the disruption to transportation resulting from ongoing conflict.

The war against the Soviet Union and the ensuing civil war also led to migration to the cities and refugee flight to Pakistan and Iran, further disrupting normal agricultural production. Recent studies indicate that agricultural production and livestock numbers are only sufficient to feed about half of Afghanistan's population. Shortages are exacerbated by the country's already limited transportation network, which has deteriorated further due to damage and neglect resulting from war and the absence of an effective central government.

Opium became a source of cash for some Afghans, especially following the breakdown in central authority after the Soviet withdrawal, and opium-derived revenues probably constituted a major source of income for the two main factions. Opium is easy to cultivate and transport and offers a quick source of income for impoverished Afghans. Afghanistan was the world's largest producer of raw opium in 1999 and 2000. In 2000 the Taliban banned opium poppy cultivation but failed to destroy the existing stockpile and presumably benefited substantially from resulting price increases. Later, in 2001, the Taliban reportedly announced that poppy cultivation could resume. Much of Afghanistan's opium production is refined into heroin and is either consumed by a growing South Asian addict population or exported, primarily to Europe.

Trade and Industry

Trade accounts for a small portion of documented Afghan economy, and there are no reliable statistics relating to trade flows. In 1996, exports, not including opium, were estimated at $80 million and imports estimated at $150 million. These figures have probably decreased over time. Since the Soviet withdrawal and the collapse of the Soviet Union, other limited trade relationships appear to be emerging with Central Asian states, Pakistan, Iran, the EU, and Japan. Afghanistan trades little with the United States. Afghanistan does not enjoy U.S. most-favored-nation (MFN) trading status, which was revoked in 1986.

Afghanistan is endowed with a wealth of natural resources, including extensive deposits of natural gas, petroleum, coal, copper, chromite, talc, barites, sulfur, lead, zinc, iron ore, salt, and precious and semiprecious stones. In the 1970s the Soviets estimated Afghanistan had as much as five trillion cubic feet (tcf) of natural gas, 95 million barrels of oil and condensate reserves, and 400 million tons of coal. Unfortunately, the country's continuing conflict, remote and rugged terrain, and inadequate transportation network usually have made mining these resources difficult, and there have been few serious attempts to further explore or exploit them.

The most important resource has been natural gas, first tapped in 1967. At their peak during the 1980s, natural gas sales accounted for $300 million a year in export revenues (56% of the total). Ninety percent of these exports went to the Soviet Union to pay for imports and debts. However, during the withdrawal o Soviet troops in 1989, Afghanistan's natural gas fields were capped to prevent sabotage by the mujahidin. Restoration of gas production has been hampered by internal strife and the disruption of traditional trading relationships following the collapse of the Soviet Union. Gas production has dropped from a high of 290 million cubic feet (Mmcf) per day in the

1980s to a current low of about 22 Mmcf in 2001.

Trade in goods smuggled into Pakistan once constituted a major source of revenue for Afghan regimes, including the Taliban, and also figured as an important element in the Afghan economy. Many of the goods smuggled into Pakistan originally entered Afghanistan from Pakistan, where they fell under the Afghan Trade and Transit Agreement (ATTA), which permitted goods bound for Afghanistan to transit Pakistan free of duty. When Pakistan clamped down in 2000 on the types of goods permitted duty-free transit, routing of goods through Iran from the Gulf increased significantly. Shipments of smuggled goods were subjected to fees and duties paid to the Afghan Government. The trade also provided jobs to tens of thousands of Afghans on both sides of the Durand Line, which forms the border between Afghanistan and Pakistan. Pakistan's closing its Afghan border in September 2001 presumably drastically curtailed this traffic.

Transportation

Landlocked Afghanistan has no functioning railways, but the Amu Darya (Oxus) River, which forms part of Afghanistan's border with Turkmenistan, Uzbekistan, and Tajikistan, has barge traffic. During their occupation of the country, the Soviets completed a bridge across the Amu Darya and built a motor vehicle and railroad bridge between Termez and Jeyretan.

Most road building occurred in the 1960s, funded by the U.S. and the Soviet Union. The Soviets built a road and tunnel through the Salang Pass in 1964, connecting northern and southern Afghanistan. A highway connecting the principal cities of Herat, Kandahar, Ghazni, and Kabul with links to highways in neighboring Pakistan formed the primary road system.

The highway system requires almost total reconstruction, and regional roads are in a state of disrepair. The poor state of the Afghan transportation and communication networks has further fragmented and hobbled the struggling economy.

Economic Development and Recovery

Afghanistan embarked on a modest economic development program in the 1930s. The government founded banks; introduced paper money; established a university; expanded primary, secondary, and technical schools; and sent students abroad for education. In 1956, the Afghan Government promulgated the first in a long series of ambitious development plans. By the late 1970s, these had achieved only mixed results due to flaws in the planning process as well as inadequate funding and a shortage of the skilled managers and technicians needed for implementation.

These constraints on development have been exacerbated by the flight of educated Afghans and the disruption and instability stemming from the Soviet occupation and ensuing civil war. Today, economic recovery and long-term development will depend on establishing an effective and stable political system and an end to more than 22 years of conflict.

The UN and the international donor community continue to provide considerable humanitarian relief. Since its inception in 1988, the umbrella UN Office for the Coordination of Humanitarian Assistance to Afghanistan (UNOCHA) has channeled more than $1 billion in multilateral assistance to Afghan refugees and vulnerable persons inside Afghanistan. The U.S., the European Union (EU), and Japan are the leading contributors to this relief effort. One of its key tasks is to eliminate from priority areas--such as villages, arable fields, and roads--some of the 5 to 7 million land mines and 750,000 pieces of unexploded ordnance, sown mainly during the Soviet occupation, which continue to litter the Afghan landscape. Afghanistan is the most heavily mined country in the world; mine-related injuries number up to 300 per month. Without successful mine clearance, refugee repatriation, political stability, and economic reconstruction will be severely constrained.

FOREIGN RELATIONS

Before the Soviet invasion, Afghanistan pursued a policy of neutrality and nonalignment in its foreign relations. In international forums, Afghanistan generally followed the voting patterns of Asian and African nonaligned countries. Following the Marxist coup of April 1978, the Taraki government developed significantly closer ties with the Soviet Union and its communist satellites.

After the December 1979 invasion, Afghanistan's foreign policy mirrored that of the Soviet Union. Afghan foreign policymakers attempted, with little success, to increase their regime's low standing in the noncommunist world. With the signing of the Geneva Accords, Najibullah unsuccessfully sought to end Afghanistan's isolation within the Islamic world and in the Non-Aligned Movement.

Most Western countries, including the United States, maintained small diplomatic missions in Kabul during the Soviet occupation. (Throughout the Soviet occupation, the U.S. did not recognize the Afghan regimes, and its mission was headed by a Charge d'Affaires rather than an Ambassador.) Many countries subsequently closed their missions due to instability and heavy fighting in Kabul.

Pakistan, Saudi Arabia, and the United Arab Emirates recognized the Taliban regime in 1997. Saudi Arabia and the UAE withdrew recognition following the September 11, 2001 bombings. Repeated Taliban efforts to occupy Afghanistan's seat at the UN and OIC were unsuccessful.

Pakistan

Two areas--Pashtunistan and Baluchistan--have long complicated Afghanistan's relations with Pakistan. Controversies involving these areas date back to the establishment of the Durand Line in 1893 dividing Pashtun and Baluch tribes living in Afghanistan from those living in what later became Pakistan. Afghanistan vigorously protested the inclusion of Pashtun and Baluch areas within Pakistan without providing the inhabitants with an opportunity for self-determination. Since 1947, this problem has led to incidents along the border, with extensive disruption of normal trade patterns. The most serious crisis lasted from September 1961 to June 1963, when diplomatic, trade, transit, and consular relations between the countries were suspended.

The 1978 Marxist coup further strained relations between the two countries. Pakistan took the lead diplomatically in the United Nations, the Non-Aligned Movement, and the Organization of the Islamic Conference in opposing the Soviet occupation. During the war against the Soviet occupation, Pakistan served as the primary logistical conduit for the Afghan resistance. Pakistan, aided by UN agencies, private groups, and many friendly countries, continues to provide refuge to several million Afghans.

Pakistan initially developed close ties to the Taliban regime, which it believed would offer strategic depth in any future conflict with India, and extended recognition in 1997. This policy was not without controversy in Pakistan, where many objected to the Taliban's human rights record and radical interpretation of Islam. Following the Taliban's resistance to Islamabad's pressure to comply with relevant UN Security Council Resolutions and surrender Usama bin Laden after the September 11 bombings in New York City and Washington, DC, Pakistan dramatically altered its policy by closing its border and downgrading its ties.

Much of Afghanistan has long relied on Pakistani links for trade and travel to the outside world, and Pakistan views Afghanistan as eventually becoming its primary route for trade with Central Asia, though these plans will of necessity await establishment of secure conditions.

Iran

Afghanistan's relations with Iran have fluctuated over the years, with periodic disputes over the water rights of the Helmand River as the main issue of contention. Following the Soviet invasion, which Iran opposed, relations deteriorated. The Iranian consulate in Herat closed, as did the Afghan consulate in Mashad. The Iranians complained of periodic border violations following the Soviet invasion. In 1985, they urged feuding Afghan Shi'a resistance groups to unite to oppose the Soviets. Iran supported the cause of the Afghan resistance and provided limited financial and military assistance to rebel leaders who pledged loyalty to the Iranian vision of Islamic revolution. Iran provides refuge to about 2 million Afghans, though it has refused to accept more in recent years and, indeed, tried to force many to repatriate.

Following the emergence of the Taliban and their harsh treatment of Afghanistan's Shi'a minority, Iran stepped up assistance to the Northern Alliance. Relations with the Taliban deteriorated further in 1998 after Taliban forces seized the Iranian consulate in Mazar-e-Sharif and executed Iranian diplomats.

Russia

In the 19th century, Afghanistan served as a strategic buffer state between czarist Russia and the British Empire in the subcontinent. Afghanistan's relations with Moscow became more cordial after the Bolshevik Revolution in 1917. The Soviet Union was the first country to establish diplomatic relations with Afghanistan after the Third Anglo-Afghan war and signed an Afghan-Soviet nonaggression pact in 1921, which also provided for Afghan transit rights through the Soviet Union. Early Soviet assistance included financial aid, aircraft and attendant technical personnel, and telegraph operators.

The Soviets began a major economic assistance program in Afghanistan in the 1950s. Between 1954 and 1978, Afghanistan received more than $1 billion in Soviet aid, including substantial military assistance. In 1973, the two countries announced a $200-million assistance agreement on gas and oil development, trade, transport, irrigation, and factory construction. Following the 1979 invasion, the Soviets augmented their large aid commitments to shore up the Afghan economy and rebuild the Afghan military. They provided the Karmal regime an unprecedented $800 million. The Soviet Union supported the Najibullah regime even after the withdrawal of Soviet troops in February 1989. Today, unresolved questions concerning Soviet MIA/POWs in Afghanistan remain an issue between Russia and Afghanistan.

Tajik rebels based in Afghanistan in July 1993 attacked a Russian border outpost in Tajikistan, killing 25 Russians and prompting Russian retaliatory strikes, which caused extensive damage in northern Afghanistan. Reports of Afghan support for the Tajik rebels have led to cool relations between the two countries.

Russia became increasingly disenchanted with the Taliban over their support for Chechen rebels and for providing a sanctuary for terrorist groups active in Central Asia and in Russia itself. Russia has provided military assistance to the Northern Alliance.

Tajikistan

Afghanistan's relations with newly independent Tajikistan have been complicated by political upheaval and civil war in Tajikistan, which spurred some 100,000 Tajiks to seek refuge in Afghanistan in late 1992 and early 1993. Tajik rebels seeking to overthrow the regime of Russian-backed former communist Imamali Rahmanov began operating from Afghan bases and recruiting Tajik refugees into their ranks. These rebels, reportedly aided by Afghans and a number of foreign Islamic extremists, conducted cross-border raids against Russian and Tajik security posts and sought to infiltrate fighters and materiel from Afghanistan into Tajikistan. Also disenchanted by the Taliban's harsh treatment of Afghanistan's Tajik minority, Tajikistan has facilitated assistance to the Northern Alliance.

U.S.-AFGHAN RELATIONS

The first extensive American contact with Afghanistan was made by Josiah Harlan, an adventurer from Pennsylvania who was an adviser in Afghan politics in the 1830s and reputedly inspired Rudyard Kipling's story "The Man Who Would be King." After the establishment of diplomatic relations in 1934, the U.S. policy of helping developing nations raise their standard of living was an important factor in maintaining and improving U.S.-Afghan ties. From 1950 to 1979, U.S. foreign assistance provided Afghanistan with more than $500 million in loans, grants, and surplus agricultural commodities to develop transportation facilities, increase agricultural production, expand the educational system, stimulate industry, and improve government administration.

In the 1950s, the U.S. declined Afghanistan's request for defense cooperation but extended an economic assistance program focused on the development of Afghanistan's physical infrastructure--roads, dams, and power plants. Later, U.S. aid shifted from infrastructure projects to technical assistance programs to help develop the skills needed to build a modern economy. The Peace Corps was active in Afghanistan between 1962 and 1979.

After the April 1978 coup, relations deteriorated. In February 1979, U.S. Ambassador Adolph "Spike" Dubs was murdered in Kabul after Afghan security forces burst in on his kidnapers. The U.S. then reduced bilateral assistance and terminated a small military training program. All remaining assistance agreements were ended after the Soviet invasion.

Following the Soviet invasion, the United States supported diplomatic efforts to achieve a Soviet withdrawal. In addition, generous U.S. contributions to the refugee program in Pakistan played a major part in efforts to assist Afghans in need. U.S. efforts also included helping Afghans living inside Afghanistan. This cross-border humanitarian assistance program aimed at increasing Afghan self-sufficiency and helping Afghans resist Soviet attempts to drive civilians out of the rebel-dominated countryside. During the period of Soviet occupation of Afghanistan, the U.S. provided about $3 billion in military and economic assistance to Afghans and the resistance movement.

The U.S. Embassy in Kabul was closed in January 1989 for security reasons. The U.S. has supported the peaceful emergence of a broad-based government representative of all Afghans and has been active in encouraging a UN role in the national reconciliation process in Afghanistan. The U.S. provides financial aid for mine-clearing activities and other humanitarian assistance to Afghans through international organizations. The U.S. is the largest provider of humanitarian assistance to Afghanistan. The aid effort has continued despite a U.S. cruise missile attack on a terrorist camp in Afghanistan associated with Usama bin Laden in 1998 and with the military action taken against terrorist and Taliban targets in October 2001.

UN EFFORTS

During the Soviet occupation, the United Nations was highly critical of the U.S.S.R.'s interference in the internal affairs of Afghanistan and was instrumental in obtaining a negotiated Soviet withdrawal under the terms of the Geneva Accords.

In the aftermath of the Accords and subsequent Soviet withdrawal, the United Nations has assisted in the repatriation of refugees and has provided humanitarian aid such as health care, educational programs, and food and has supported mine-clearing operations. The UNDP and associated agencies have undertaken a limited number of development projects. However, the UN reduced its role in Afghanistan in 1992 in the wake of fierce factional strife in and around Kabul. The UN Secretary General has designated a personal representative to head the Office for the Coordination of Humanitarian Assistance to Afghanistan (UNOCHA) and the Special Mission to Afghanistan (UNSMA), both based in Islamabad, Pakistan. Throughout the late 1990s, 2000, and 2001, the UN unsuccessfully strived to promote a peaceful settlement between the Afghan factions as well as provide humanitarian aid, this despite increasing Taliban restrictions upon UN personnel and agencies.

TRAVEL AND BUSINESS INFORMATION

The U.S. Department of State's Consular Information Program provides Consular Information Sheets, Travel Warnings, and Public Announcements. **Consular Information Sheets** exist for all countries and include information on entry requirements, currency regulations, health conditions, areas of instability, crime and security, political disturbances, and the addresses of the U.S. posts in the country. **Travel Warnings** are issued when the State Department recommends that Americans avoid travel to a certain country. **Public

Announcements are issued as a means to disseminate information quickly about terrorist threats and other relatively short-term conditions overseas which pose significant risks to the security of American travelers. Free copies of this information are available by calling the Bureau of Consular Affairs at 202-647-5225 or via the fax-on-demand system: 202-647-3000. Consular Information Sheets and Travel Warnings also are available on the Consular Affairs Internet home page: **http://travel.state.gov**. Consular Affairs Tips for Travelers publication series, which contain information on obtaining passports and planning a safe trip abroad are on the internet and hard copies can be purchased from the Superintendent of Documents, U.S. Government Printing Office, telephone: 202-512-1800; fax 202-512-2250.

Emergency information concerning Americans traveling abroad may be obtained from the Office of Overseas Citizens Services at (202) 647-5225. For after-hours emergencies, Sundays and holidays, call 202-647-4000.

Passport information can be obtained by calling the National Passport Information Center's automated system ($.35 per minute) or live operators 8 a.m. to 8 p.m. (EST) Monday-Friday ($1.05 per minute). The number is 1-900-225-5674 (TDD: 1-900-225-7778). Major credit card users (for a flat rate of $4.95) may call 1-888-362-8668 (TDD: 1-888-498-3648). It also is available on the internet.

Travelers can check the latest health information with the U.S. Centers for Disease Control and Prevention in Atlanta, Georgia. A hotline at 877-FYI-TRIP (877-394-8747) and a web site at **http://www.cdc.gov/travel/index.htm** give the most recent health advisories, immunization recommendations or requirements, and advice on food and drinking water safety for regions and countries. A booklet entitled Health Information for International Travel (HHS publication number CDC-95-8280) is available from the U.S. Government Printing Office, Washington, DC 20402, tel. (202) 512-1800.

Information on travel conditions, visa requirements, currency and customs regulations, legal holidays, and other items of interest to travelers also may be obtained before your departure from a country's embassy and/or consulates in the U.S. (for this country, see "Principal Government Officials" listing in this publication).

U.S. citizens who are long-term visitors or traveling in dangerous areas are encouraged to register at the U.S. embassy upon arrival in a country (see "Principal U.S. Embassy Officials" listing in this publication). This may help family members contact you in case of an emergency.

Further Electronic Information

Department of State Web Site. Available on the Internet at **http://state.gov**, the Department of State web site provides timely, global access to official U.S. foreign policy information, including **Background Notes**; **daily press briefings**; **Country Commercial Guides**; directories of key officers of Foreign Service posts and more.

National Trade Data Bank (NTDB). Operated by the U.S. Department of Commerce, the NTDB contains a wealth of trade-related information. It is available on the Internet (**www.stat-usa.gov**) and on CD-ROM. Call the NTDB Help-Line at (202) 482-1986 for more information.

The **LIBRARY** *of* **CONGRESS**

Country Studies

This website contains the on-line versions of books previously published in hard copy by the Federal Research Division of the Library of Congress under the Country Studies/Area Handbook Program sponsored by the U.S. Department of Army. Because the original intent of the Series' sponsor was to focus primarily on lesser known areas of the world or regions in which U.S. forces might be deployed, the series is not all-inclusive. At present, 101 countries and regions are covered. Notable omissions include Canada, France, the United Kingdom, and other Western nations, as well as a number of African nations. The date of information for each country appears on the title page of each country and at the end of each section of text.

About the Country Studies/Area Handbooks Program

The Country Studies Series presents a description and analysis of the historical setting and the social, economic, political, and national security systems and institutions of countries throughout the world and examines the interrelationships of those systems and the ways they are shaped by cultural factors.

The books represent the analysis of the authors and should not be construed as an expression of an official United States Government position, policy, or decision. The authors have sought to adhere to accepted standards of scholarly objectivity. Corrections, additions, and suggestions for changes from readers will be welcomed for use in future hard copy editions (E-mail frds@loc.gov).

Information contained in the Country Studies On-Line is not copyrighted and thus is available for free and unrestricted use by researchers. As a courtesy, however, appropriate credit should be given to the series.

Hard copy editions of all books in the series (except the regional study on Macau) can be ordered from Claitor's Publishing Div., PO Box 261333, Baton Rouge, LA 70826-1333; On the web at www.claitors.com; by phone 800-274-1403.

Features Note:

Some countries lack graphic information because graphic files were not available or have not yet been converted for mounting on this site. Where appropriate links to graphics have been added, the names of the countries appear in **bold type-face** in thelist of countries below.

New Country Studies:

Countries may be added without the photographs, maps, and charts. When all appropriate links have been added, the countries will appear in **bold type-face**.

Note on Timeliness:

Studies included here were published between 1988 and 1998. Information on some countries may no longer be up to date. See the "Research Completed" date at the beginning of each study or the "Data as of" date at the end of each section of text. Older studies, including some on countries that no longer exist in the same form, such as East Germany and the Soviet Union, may be retained because they continue to offer historical information of value to researchers.

Browse Table of Country Studies

*Hardbound unless indicated otherwise

- Afghanistan(paper) $35
- Albania $28
- Algeria...................................... $25
- American Samoa -*see Oceania*
- Angola $26
- Antiqua - *see Commonwealth of Caribbean Islands*
- Armenia,Azerbaijan, and Georgia $39
- Austria $24
- Azerbaijan- *see Armenia*
- Bahamas - *see Commonwealth of Caribbean Islands*
- Bahrain - *see Persian Gulf States*
- Bangladesh $26
- Barbados -*see Commonwealth of Caribbean Islands*
- Barbuda -*see Commonwealth of Caribbean Islands*
- Belarus and Moldova $22
- Belize - *see Guyana*
- Bhutan - *see Nepal*
- Bolivia $29
- Brazil $42
- Bulgaria $34
- Cambodia $29
- Chad $25
- Chile $32
- China $44
- Colombia $29
- Commonwealth of Caribbean Islands: A regional study of Jamaica, Trinidad, Tobago, Dominica, St. Lucia, St. Vincent, Grenadines, Grenada, Barbados, Antigua, Barbuda, St. Christopher, Nevis, Bahamas, and Commonwealth of British Dependencies $50
- Commonwealth of British Dependencies - *see Commonwealth of Caribbean Islands*
- Comoros - *see Indian Ocean*
- Cuba $28
- Cyprus...................................... $29
- Czechoslovakia (former) $29
- Dominica - *see Commonwealth of Caribbean Islands*
- Dominican Republic and Haiti $33
- Ecuador $26
- Egypt $33
- El Salvador $26
- Estonia, Latvia, and Lithuania $29
- Ethiopia..................................... $34
- Finland $33
- Georgia - *see Armenia*
- Germany $50
- Germany (East) $35

Ghana $26
Greece $28
Grenada - *see Commonwealth of the Caribbean Islands*
Grenadines - *see Commonwealth of the Caribbean Islands*
Guam - *see Oceania*
Guyana and Belize $31
Haiti - *see Dominican Republic*
Honduras $24
Hungary $24
India $59
Indian Ocean: Five Island Countries Maldives, Madagascar,
    Mauritius, Comoros and Seychelles $28
Indonesia $40
Iran $20
Iraq $26
Israel $32
Italy $20
Ivory Coast (Cote d'Ivoire) $25
Japan $43
Jamaica - *see Commonwealth of Caribbean Islands*
Jordan $28
Kazakstan, Kyrgyzstan, Tajikistan, Turkmenistan and
    Uzbekistan $42
Kuwait - *see Persian Gulf States*
Kyrgyzstan - *see Kazakstan*
Latvia - *see Estonia*
Laos $26
Lebanon $25
Liberia $18
Libya $32
Lithuania - *see Estonia*
Macau $35
Madagascar - *see Indian Ocean*
Malaysia $18
Maldives - *see Indian Ocean*
Mauritania $23
Mauritius - *see Indian Ocean*
Melanesia - *see Oceania*
Mexico $32
Micronesia - *see Oceania*
Moldova - *see Belarus*
Mongolia $28
Morocco $25
Mozambique $20
Nepal and Bhutan $35
Nevis - *see Commonwealth of Caribbean Islands*
Nicaragua $23
Nigeria $34
North Korea $29
Oceania: A Regional Study of Melanesia, Micronesia,
    Polynesia, Guam, and American Samoa $26
Oman - *see Persian Gulf States*

- Pakistan $28
- Panama $28
- Paraguay $26
- Persian Gulf States: Kuwait, Bahrain, Qatar, United Arab Emirates and Oman $32
- Peru $36
- Philippines $35
- Poland $33
- Polynesia - *see Oceania*
- Portugal $28
- Qatar - *see Persian Gulf States*
- Romania $28
- Russia $48
- Saudi Arabia $32
- Seychelles - *see Indian Ocean*
- Singapore $28
- Somalia $28
- South Africa $41
- South Korea $34
- Soviet Union (former) $59
- Spain $33
- Sri Lanka $25
- St. Christopher - *see Commonwealth of Caribbean Islands*
- St. Lucia - *see Commonwealth of Caribbean Islands*
- St. Vincent - *see Commonwealth of Caribbean Islands*
- Sudan $31
- Syria $26
- Tajikistan- *see Kazakstan*
- Thailand $29
- Tobago - *see Commonwealth of Caribbean Islands*
- Trinidad - *see Commonwealth of Caribbean Islands*
- Tunisia $22
- Turkmenistan - *see Kazakstan*
- Turkey $31
- Uganda $28
- United Arab Emirates - *see Persian Gulf States*
- Uruguay $29
- Uzbekistan- *see Kazakstan*
- Venezuela $28
- Vietnam $29
- Yugoslavia (former) $32
- Zaire $28
- Zimbabwe $10

Contents

Foreword V
Background Notes VII
Library of Congress Country Studies XXXVII
Table of Country Studies XXXIX

CHAPTER 1. HISTORICAL SETTING 1
Craig Baxter

THE PRE-ISLAMIC PERIOD 5
    Achaemenid Rule, ca. 550-331 B.C. 5
    Alexander and Greek Rule, 330-ca. 150 B.C. 6
    Central Asian and Sassanian Rule, ca. 150 B.C.-700 A.D. 7
ISLAMIC CONQUEST 11
    Ghaznavid and Ghorid Rule 12
    Mongol Rule, 1220-1506 13
    Mughal-Safavid Rivalry, ca. 1500-1747 13
AHMAD SHAH AND THE DURRANI EMPIRE 17
THE GREAT GAME 23
    The Rise of Dost Mohammad 23
    The First Anglo-Afghan War 26
    The Second Anglo-Afghan War 28
ABDUR RAHMAN KHAN, "THE IRON AMIR," 1880-1901 . 31
    Consolidation of the Modern State 31
    Modernization and Development of Institutions 32
THE REIGN OF KING HABIBULLAH, 1901-1919 37
THE REIGN OF KING AMANULLAH, 1919-29 41
    Third Anglo-Afghan War and Independence 41
    Reform, Popular Reaction, and Forced Abdication 43
TAJIK RULE, JANUARY-OCTOBER 1929 47
MUHAMMAD NADIR SHAH, 1929-33 51
MOHAMMAD ZAHIR SHAH, 1933-73 55
    Zahir Shah and His Uncles, 1933-53 55
    The Pashtunistan Issue 57
    Early Links with the Soviet Union 58
    Experiment with Liberalized Politics 59

Daoud as Prime Minister, 1953-63 60
The King Reigns: The Last Decade of the Monarchy,
1963-73 63
DAOUD'S REPUBLIC, JULY 1973- APRIL 1978 69
COMMUNISM, REBELLION, AND SOVIET
INTERVENTION 73

CHAPTER 2. THE SOCIETY AND ITS ENVIRONMENT . . 83
Nancy Hatch Dupree and Thomas E. Gouttierre

THE NATURAL ENVIRONMENT 89
Mountains 89
Rivers 92
Regions 92
Climate 94
POPULATION 99
SOCIAL STRUCTURE 103
Ethnic Groups 104
Pashtun 104
Tajik 106
Hazara 108
Uzbek 109
Turkmen 110
Other Groups 111
Aimaq 111
Arab 111
Kirghiz 112
Wakhi 112
Farsiwan 113
Nuristani 113
Baluch 114
Brahui 114
Qizilbash 115
Kabuli 116
Jat 117
Non-Muslims 117
Interethnic Relations 118

Tribes 121
MODES OF SUBSISTENCE 125
Pastoralism 125
Mixed Subsistence Patterns 128
FAMILY 131
GENDER ROLES 141
RELIGION 147
Early Development of Islam 147
Sunni and Shia Islam 148
Sufism 149
Tenets of Islam 151
Islamic Expression in Afghanistan 154
Sunnis of the Hanafi School 155
Ithna Ashariya (Twelver or Imami) Shia 155
Ismailis 156
Sufis 157
Meaning and Practice 159
Politicized Islam 163
EDUCATION 169
Literacy 170
Administrative Structure 171
Enrollment 171
Curriculum 172
Teacher Training 173
Higher Education 173
Adult Literacy 174
Current Activities 175
HEALTH 179
REFUGEES AND REPATRIATION 183
WARFARE AND CIVIC CULTURE 189
Index 195
Extract on Afghanistan(World Factbook 2001) 205

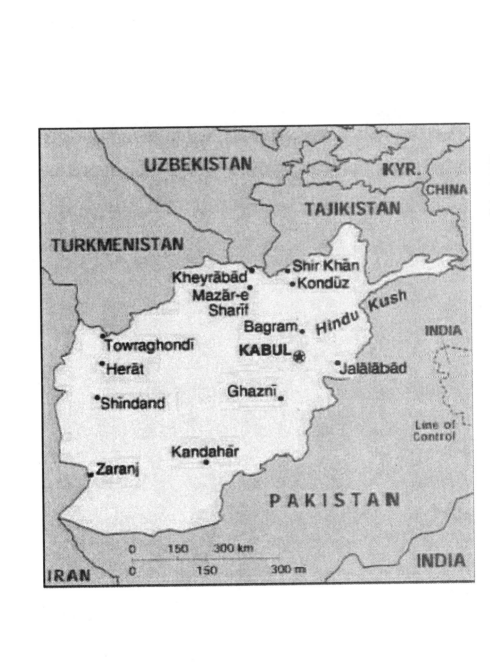

CHAPTER 1.
HISTORICAL SETTING

AFGHANISTAN'S HISTORY, internal political development, foreign relations, and very existence as an independent state have largely been determined by its geographic location at the crossroads of Central, West, and South Asia. Over the centuries, waves of migrating peoples passed through the region--described as a "roundabout of the ancient world," by historian Arnold Toynbee--leaving behind a mosaic of ethnic and linguistic groups. In modern times, as well as in antiquity, vast armies of the world passed through Afghanistan, temporarily establishing local control and often dominating Iran and northern India.

Although it was the scene of great empires and flourishing trade for over two millennia, Afghanistan did not become a truly independent nation until the twentieth century. The area's heterogeneous groups were not bound into a single political entity until the reign of Ahmad Shah Durrani, who in 1747 founded the monarchy that ruled the country until 1973. In the nineteenth century, Afghanistan lay between the expanding might of the Russian and British empires. In 1900, Abdur Rahman Khan (the "Iron Amir"), looking back on his twenty years of rule and the events of the past century, wondered how his country, which stood "like a goat between these lions [Britain and Tsarist Russia] or a grain of wheat between two strong millstones of the grinding mill, [could] stand in the midway of the stones without being ground to dust?" Constrained by the competing dictates of powerful British and Russian empires, Abdur Rahman focused instead on consolidating his power within Afghanistan and creating the institutions of a modern nation-state.

Islam played a key role in the formation of Afghan history as well. Despite the Mongol invasion of Afghanistan in the early thirteenth century which has been described as resembling "more some brute cataclysm of the blind forces of nature than a phenomenon of human history," even a warrior as formidable as Genghis Khan did not uproot Islamic civilization, and within two generations his heirs had become Muslims. An often

2

unacknowledged event that nevertheless played an important role in Afghan history (and in the politics of Afghanistan's neighbors and the entire region up to the present) was the rise in the tenth century of a strong Sunni dynasty--the Ghaznavids. Their power prevented the eastward spread of Shiism from Iran, thereby insuring that the majority of the Muslims in Afghanistan and South Asia would be Sunnis.

THE PRE-ISLAMIC PERIOD

Archaeological exploration began in Afghanistan in earnest after World War II and proceeded promisingly until the Soviet invasion disrupted it in December of 1979. Artifacts typical of the Paleolithic, Mesolithic, Neolithic, Bronze, and Iron ages were found. It is not yet clear, however, to what extent these periods were contemporaneous with similar stages of development in other geographic regions. The area that is now Afghanistan seems in prehistory--as well as ancient and modern times--to have been closely connected by culture and trade with the neighboring regions to the east, west, and north. Urban civilization in the Iranian plateau, which includes most of Iran and Afghanistan, may have begun as early as 3000 to 2000 B.C. About the middle of the second millennium B.C. people speaking an Indo-European language may have entered the eastern part of the Iranian Plateau, but little is known about the area until the middle of the first millennium B.C., when its history began to be recorded during the Achaemenid Empire.

Achaemenid Rule, ca. 550-331 B.C.

The area that is present-day Afghanistan comprised several satrapies (provinces) of the Achaemenid Empire when it was at its most extensive, under Darius the Great (ca. 500 B.C.). Bactriana, with its capital at Bactria (which later became Balkh), was reputedly the home of Zoroaster, who founded the religion that bears his name.

By the fourth century B.C., Iranian control of outlying areas and the internal cohesion of the empire had become tenuous. Although outlying areas like Bactriana had always been restless under Achaemenid rule, Bactrian troops nevertheless fought on the Iranian side in the decisive Battle of Gaugamela (330 B.C.). They were defeated by Alexander the Great.

Alexander and Greek Rule, 330-ca. 150 B.C.

It took Alexander only three years (from about 330-327 B.C.) to subdue the area that is now Afghanistan and the adjacent regions of the former Soviet Union. Moving eastward from the area of Herat, the Macedonian leader encountered fierce resistance from local rulers of what had been Iranian satraps. Although his expedition through Afghanistan was brief, he left behind a Hellenic cultural influence that lasted several centuries.

Upon Alexander's death in 323 B.C., his empire, which had never been politically consolidated, broke apart. His cavalry commander, Seleucus, took nominal control of the eastern lands and founded the Seleucid dynasty. Under the Seleucids, as under Alexander, Greek colonists and soldiers entered the region of the Hindu Kush, and many are believed to have remained. At the same time, the Mauryan Empire was developing in the northern part of the Indian subcontinent. It took control, thirty years after Alexander's death, of the southeasternmost areas of the Seleucid domains, including parts of present-day Afghanistan. The Mauryans introduced Indian culture, including Buddhism, to the area. With the Seleucids on one side and the Mauryans on the other, the people of the Hindu Kush were in what would become a familiar quandary in ancient as well as modern history--that is, caught between two empires.

In the middle of the third century B.C., an independent, Greek-ruled state was declared in Bactria. Graeco-Bactrian rule spread until it included most of the territory from the Iranian deserts to the Ganges River and from Central Asia to the Arabian Sea by about 170 B.C. Graeco-Bactrian rule was eventually defeated by a combination of the internecine disputes that plagued Greek rulers to the west, the ambitious attempts to extend control into northern India, and the pressure of two groups of nomadic invaders from Central Asia--the Parthians and Sakas (perhaps the Scythians).

Central Asian and Sassanian Rule, ca. 150 B.C.-700 A.D.

In the third and second centuries B.C., the Parthians, a nomadic people speaking Indo-European languages, arrived on the Iranian Plateau. The Parthians established control in most of what is Iran as early as the middle of the third century B.C.; about 100 years later another Indo-European group from the north--the Kushans (a subgroup of the tribe called the Yuezhi by the Chinese)--entered Afghanistan and established an empire lasting almost four centuries.

The Kushan Empire spread from the Kabul River Valley to defeat other Central Asian tribes that had previously conquered parts of the northern central Iranian Plateau once ruled by the Parthians. By the middle of the first century B.C., the Kushans' control stretched from the Indus Valley to the Gobi Desert and as far west as the central Iranian Plateau. Early in the second century A.D. under Kanishka, the most powerful of the Kushan rulers, the empire reached its greatest geographic and cultural breadth to become a center of literature and art. Kanishka extended Kushan control to the mouth of the Indus River on the Arabian Sea, into Kashmir, and into what is today the Chinese-controlled area north of Tibet. Kanishka was a patron of religion and the arts. It was during his reign that Mahayana Buddhism, imported to northern India earlier by the Mauryan emperor Ashoka (ca. 260-232 B.C.), reached its zenith in Central Asia.

In the third century A.D., Kushan control fragmented into semi-independent kingdoms that became easy targets for conquest by the rising Iranian dynasty, the Sassanians (ca. 224-561 A.D.). These small kingdoms were pressed by both the Sassanians from the west and by the growing strength of the Guptas, an Indian dynasty established at the beginning of the fourth century.

The disunited Kushan and Sassanian kingdoms were in a poor position to meet the threat of a new wave of nomadic, Indo-European invaders from the north. The Hepthalites (or White

Huns) swept out of Central Asia around the fourth century into Bactria and to the south, overwhelming the last of the Kushan and Sassanian kingdoms. Historians believe that their control continued for a century and was marked by constant warfare with the Sassanians to the west.

By the middle of the sixth century the Hepthalites were defeated in the territories north of the Amu Darya (the Oxus River of antiquity) by another group of Central Asian nomads, the Western Turks, and by the resurgent Sassanians in the lands south of the Amu Darya. Up until the advent of Islam, the lands of the Hindu Kush were dominated up to the Amu Darya by small kingdoms under Sassanian control but with local rulers who were Kushans or Hepthalites.

Of this great Buddhist culture and earlier Zoroastrian influence there remain few, if any, traces in the life of Afghan people today. Along ancient trade routes, however, stone monuments of Buddhist culture exist as reminders of the past. The two great sandstone Buddhas, thirty-five and fifty-three meters high overlook the ancient route through Bamian to Balkh and date from the third and fifth centuries A.D. In this and other key places in Afghanistan, archaeologists have located frescoes, stucco decorations, statuary, and rare objects from China, Phoenicia, and Rome crafted as early as the second century A.D. that bear witness to the influence of these ancient civilizations on the arts in Afghanistan.

[RESERVED]

ISLAMIC CONQUEST

In 637 A.D., only five years after the death of the Prophet Muhammad, Arab Muslims shattered the might of the Iranian Sassanians at the battle of Qadisiya, and the invaders began to reach into the lands east of Iran. By the middle of the eighth century, the rising Abbasid Dynasty was able to subdue the Arab invasion, putting an end to the prolonged struggle. Peace prevailed under the rule of the caliph Harun al Rashid (785-809) and his son, and learning flourished in such Central Asian cities as Samarkand. From the seventh through the ninth centuries, most inhabitants of what is present-day Afghanistan, Pakistan, southern parts of the former Soviet Union, and areas of northern India were converted to Sunni Islam.

In the eighth and ninth centuries ancestors of many of today's Turkic-speaking Afghans settled in the Hindu Kush area (partly to obtain better grazing land) and began to assimilate much of the culture and language of the Pashtun tribes already present there *(see Ethnic Groups, ch. 2)*

By the middle of the ninth century, Abbasid rule had faltered, and semi-independent states began to emerge throughout the empire. In the Hindu Kush area, three short-lived, local dynasties ascended to power. The best known of the three, the Samanid, extended its rule from Bukhara as far south as India and west as Iran. Although Arab Muslim intellectual life still was centered in Baghdad, Iranian Muslim scholarship, that is, Shia Islam, predominated in the Samanid areas at this time. By the mid-tenth century, the Samanid Dynasty had crumbled in the face of attacks from Turkish tribes to the north and from the Ghaznavids, a rising dynasty to the south.

Ghaznavid and Ghorid Rule

Out of the Samanid Dynasty came the first great Islamic empire in Afghanistan, the Ghaznavid, whose warriors, raiding deep into the Indian subcontinent, assured the domination of Sunni Islam in what is now Afghanistan, Pakistan, and parts of India. The most renowned of the dynasty's rulers was Mahmud, who consolidated control over the areas south of the Amu Darya then carried out devastating raids into India--looting Hindu temples and seeking converts to Islam. With his booty from India, he built a great capital at Ghazni, founded universities, and patronized scholars. Mahmud was recognized by the caliph in Baghdad as the temporal heir of the Samanids. By the time of his death, Mahmud ruled the entire Hindu Kush region as far east as the Punjab as well as territories far north of the Amu Darya. However, as occurred so often in this region, the demise in 1130 of this military genius who had expanded the empire to its farthest reaches was the death knell of the dynasty itself. The rulers of the Kingdom of Ghor, southeast of Herat, captured and burned Ghazni, just as the Ghaznavids had once conquered Ghor. Not until 1186, however, was the last representative of the Ghaznavids uprooted by the Ghorids from his holdout in the Punjab.

The Ghorids controlled most of what is now Afghanistan, eastern Iran, and Pakistan, while parts of central and western Iran were ruled by the Seljuk Turks. Around 1200, most Ghorid lands came into the hands of the Khwarazm Turks who had invaded from Central Asia across the Amu Darya.

Mongol Rule, 1220-1506

In 1220, the Islamic lands of Central Asia were overrun by the armies of the Mongol invader Genghis Khan (ca. 1155-1227), who laid waste to many civilizations and created an empire that stretched from China to the Caspian Sea. But he failed to destroy the strength of Islam in Central Asia. In fact, by the end of the thirteenth century, Genghis Khan's descendants had themselves become Muslims. From the death of Genghis Khan in 1227 until the rise of Timur (Tamerlane) in the 1380s, Central Asia went through a period of fragmentation.

A product of both Turkish and Mongol descent, Timur claimed Genghis Khan as an ancestor. From his capital of Samarkand, Timur created an empire that, by the late fourteenth century, extended from India to Turkey. The turn of the sixteenth century brought an end to Timurid Empire when another Mongol-Turkish ruler overwhelmed the weak Timurid ruler in Herat. Muhammad Shaybani (also a descendant of Genghis Khan) and his successors ruled the area around the Amu Darya for about a century, while to the south and west of what is now Afghanistan two powerful dynasties began to compete for influence.

Mughal-Safavid Rivalry, ca. 1500-1747

Early in the sixteenth century, Babur, who was descended from Timur on his father's side and from Genghis Khan on his mother's, was driven out of his father's kingdom in the Ferghana Valley (which straddles contemporary Uzbekistan, Tajikistan and Kyrgyzstan) by the Shaybani Uzbeks, who had wrested Samarkand from the Timurids. After several unsuccessful attempts to regain Ferghana and Samarkand, Babur crossed the Amu Darya and captured Kabul from the last of its Mongol rulers in 1504. In his invasion of India in 1526, Babur's army of 12,000 defeated a less mobile force of 100,000 at the First Battle of Panipat, about forty-five kilometers northwest of Delhi. Although the seat of the great Mughal Empire he founded was in India, Babur's memoirs stressed his love for Kabul--both as a commercial strategic center as well as a beautiful highland city with an "extremely delightful" climate.

Although Indian Mughal rule technically lasted until the nineteenth century, its days of power extended from 1526 until the death of Babur's great-great-great-grandson, Aurangzeb in 1707. The Mughals originally had come from Central Asia, but once they had taken India, the area that is now Afghanistan was relegated to a mere outpost of the empire. Indeed, during the sixteenth and seventeenth centuries, most of the Hindu Kush area was hotly contested between the Mughals of India and the powerful Safavids of Iran. Just as Kabul dominates the high road from Central Asia into India, Qandahar commands the only approach to India that skirts the Hindu Kush. The strategically important Kabul-Qandahar axis was the primary forces of competition between the Mughals and the Safavids, and Qandahar itself changed hands several times during the sixteenth and seventeenth centuries. The Safavids and the Mughals were not the only contenders, however. Less powerful but closer at hand were the Uzbeks of Central Asia, who fought for control of Herat in western Afghanistan and for the northern regions as well where neither the Mughals nor the Safavids were in strength.

The Mughals sought not only to block the historical western invasion routes into India but also to control the fiercely independent tribes who accepted only nominal control from Delhi in their mountain strongholds between the Kabul-Qandahar axis and the Indus River--especially in the Pashtun area of the Suleiman mountain range. As the area around Qandahar changed hands back and forth between the two great empires on either side, the local Pashtun tribes exploited the situation to their advantage by extracting concessions from both sides. By the middle of the seventeenth century, the Mughals had abandoned the Hindu Kush north of Kabul to the Uzbeks, and in 1748 they lost Qandahar to the Safavids for the third and final time.

Toward the end of the seventeenth century, as the power of both the Safavids and the Mughals waned, new groups began to assert themselves in the Hindu Kush area. Early in the eighteenth century, one of the Pashtun tribes, the Hotaki, seized Qandahar from the Safavids, and a group of Ghilzai Pashtuns subsequently made greater inroads into Safavid territory. The Ghilzai Pashtuns (see_____, ch. 2) even managed briefly to hold the Safavid capital of Isfahan, and two members of this tribe ascended the throne before the Ghilzai were evicted from Iran by a warrior, Nadir Shah, who became known as the "Persian Napoleon."

Nadir Shah conquered Qandahar and Kabul in 1738 along with defeating a great Mughal army in India, plundering Delhi, and massacring thousands of its people. He returned home with vast treasures, including the Peacock Throne, which thereafter served as a symbol of Iranian imperial might.

AHMAD SHAH AND THE DURRANI EMPIRE

From Nadir Shah's death in 1747 until the communist coup of April 1978, Afghanistan was governed--at least nominally--by Pashtun rulers from the Abdali group of clans. Indeed, it was under the leadership of the first Pashtun ruler, Ahmad Shah, that the nation of Afghanistan began to take shape following centuries of fragmentation and exploitation. Even before the death of Nadir Shah, tribes in the Hindu Kush had been growing stronger and were beginning to take advantage of the waning power of their distant rulers. Two lineage groups within the Abdali ruled Afghanistan from 1747 until the downfall of the monarchy in the 1970s--the Sadozai of the Popalzai tribe, and the Muhammadzai of the Barakzai tribe.

In 1747 Ahmad Shah and his Abdali horsemen joined the chiefs of the Abdali tribes and clans near Qandahar to choose a leader. Despite being younger than other claimants, Ahmad had several overriding factors in his favor. He was a direct descendant of Sado, eponym of the Sadozai; he was unquestionably a charismatic leader and seasoned warrior who had at his disposal a trained, mobile force of several thousand cavalrymen; and he possessed part of Nadir Shah's treasury.

One of Ahmad Shah's first acts as chief was to adopt the title "Durr-i-Durrani" ("pearl of pearls" or "pearl of the age"), which may have come from a dream or from the pearl earrings worn by the royal guard of Nadir Shah. The Abdali Pashtuns were known thereafter as the Durrani.

Ahmad Shah began by capturing Ghazni from the Ghilzai Pashtuns, and then wresting Kabul from the local ruler. In 1749 the Mughal ruler ceded sovereignty over Sindh Province and the areas of northern India west of the Indus to Ahmad Shah in order to save his capital from Afghan attack. Ahmad Shah then set out westward to take possession of Herat, which was ruled by Nadir Shah's grandson, Shah Rukh. Herat fell to Ahmad after almost a year of siege and bloody conflict, as did Mashhad (in present-day Iran). Ahmad next sent an army to subdue the areas north of the Hindu Kush. In short order, the powerful army brought under its control the Turkmen, Uzbek, Tajik, and Hazara tribes of northern Afghanistan (see Ethnic Groups, ch. 2). Ahmad invaded India a third, then a fourth, time, taking control of the Punjab, Kashmir, and the city of Lahore. Early in 1757, he sacked Delhi, but permitted the Mughal Dynasty to remain in nominal control as long as the ruler acknowledged Ahmad's suzerainty over the Punjab, Sindh, and Kashmir. Leaving his second son Timur in charge, Ahmad left India to return to Afghanistan.

The collapse of Mughal control in India, however, also facilitated the rise of rulers other than Ahmad Shah. In the Punjab, the Sikhs were becoming a potent force. From their capital at Pune, the Marathas, Hindus who controlled much of western and central India, were beginning to look northward to the decaying Mughal empire, which Ahmad Shah now claimed by conquest. Upon his return to Qandahar in 1757, Ahmad faced Maratha attacks which succeeded in ousting Timur and his court in India.

Ahmad Shah declared an Islamic holy war against the Marathas, and warriors from various Pashtun tribes, as well as other tribes such as the Baloch, answered his call. Early skirmishes ended in victory for the Afghans, and by 1759 Ahmad and his army had reached Lahore. By 1760 the Maratha groups had coalesced into a great army. Once again Panipat was the scene of a confrontation between two warring contenders for control of northern India. The Battle of Panipat in 1761 between Muslim and Hindu armies who numbered as many as 100,000 troops each was fought along a twelve-kilometer front. Despite decisively defeating the Marathas, what might have been Ahmad Shah's peaceful control of his domains was disrupted by other challenges.

The victory at Panipat was the high point of Ahmad Shah's--and Afghan--power. Afterward, even prior to his death, the empire began to unravel. By the end of 1761, the Sikhs had gained power and taken control of much of the Punjab. In 1762 Ahmad Shah crossed the passes from Afghanistan for the sixth time to subdue the Sikhs. He assaulted Lahore and, after taking their holy city of Amritsar, massacred thousands of Sikh inhabitants, destroying their temples and desecrating their holy places with cow's blood. Within two years the Sikhs rebelled again. Ahmad Shah tried several more times to subjugate the Sikhs permanently, but failed. By the time of his death, he had lost all but nominal control of the Punjab to the Sikhs, who remained in charge of the area until the British defeat in 1849.

Ahmad Shah also faced other rebellions in the north, and eventually he and the amir of Bukhara agreed that the Amu Darya would mark the division of their lands. In 1772 Ahmad Shah retired to his home in the mountains east of Qandahar, where he died. Ahmad Shah had succeeded to a remarkable degree in balancing tribal alliances and hostilities and in directing tribal energies away from rebellion. He earned recognition as Ahmad Shah Baba, or "Father" of Afghanistan (fig. _, Ahmad Shah Durrani's Empire, 1762).

By the time of Ahmad Shah's ascendancy, the Pashtuns included many groups whose origins were obscure; most were believed to have descended from ancient Aryan tribes, but some, such as the Ghilzai, may have once been Turks (see Ethnic Groups, ch. 2). They had in common, however, their Pashtu language. To the east, the Waziris and their close relatives, the Mahsuds, had lived in the hills of the central Suleiman Range since the fourteenth century. By the end of the sixteenth century and the final Turkish-Mongol invasions, tribes such as the Shinwaris, Yusufzais, and Mohmands had moved from the upper Kabul River Valley into the valleys and plains west, north, and northeast of Peshawar. The Afridis had long been established in the hills and mountain ranges south of the Khyber Pass. By the end of the eighteenth century, the Durranis had blanketed the area west and north of Qandahar.

Ahmad Shah's successors governed so ineptly during a period of profound unrest that within fifty years of his death, Afghanistan was embroiled in a civil war. Many of the territories conquered with the help of Ahmad Shah's military skill fell to others in this half century. By 1818 the Sadozai rulers who succeeded Ahmad Shah controlled little more than Kabul and the surrounding territory within a 160-kilometer radius. They not only lost the outlying territories but also alienated other tribes and lineages among the Durrani Pashtuns.

After the death of Ahmad Shah's successor, Timur, the three strongest contenders for the position of shah were Timur's sons, the governors of Qandahar, Herat, and Kabul. Muhammad Zeman, governor of Kabul, was in the most commanding position and became shah at the age of twenty-three. His half-brothers accepted this only by force majeure--upon being imprisoned on their arrival in the capital for the purpose, ironically, of electing a new shah. The quarrels among Timur's descendants that threw Afghanistan into turmoil also provided the pretext for the intervention of outside forces.

The efforts of the Sadozai heirs of Timur to impose a true monarchy on the truculent Pashtun tribes and to rule absolutely and without the advice of the other, larger Pashtun tribes' leaders were ultimately unsuccessful. The Sikhs too, were particularly troublesome, and after several unsuccessful efforts to subdue them, Zeman made the mistake of appointing a forceful young Sikh chief, Ranjit Singh, as his governor in the Punjab. The "one-eyed" warrior would later become an implacable enemy of Pashtun rulers in Afghanistan.

Zeman's downfall was triggered by his attempts to consolidate power. Although it had been through the support of the Muhammadzai chief, Painda Khan, that he had come to the throne, Zeman soon began to remove prominent Muhammadzai leaders from positions of power and replacing them with men of his own lineage, the Sadozai. This upset the delicate balance of Durrani tribal politics that Ahmad Shah had established and may have prompted Painda Khan and other Durrani chiefs to plot against the shah. Painda Khan and the chiefs of the Nurzai and the Alizai Durrani clans were executed, as was the chief of the Qizilbash clan. Painda Khan's son fled to Iran and pledged the substantial support of his Muhammadzai followers to a rival claimant to the throne, Zeman's older brother, Mahmud. The clans of the chiefs Zeman had executed joined forces with the rebels, and they took Qandahar without bloodshed.

Zeman's overthrow in 1800 was not the end of civil strife in Afghanistan but the beginning of even greater violence. Shah Mahmud reigned for a mere three years before being replaced by yet another of Timur Shah's sons, Shuja, who ruled for only six years, from 1803 to 1809. On June 7, 1809, Shuja signed a Treaty of Friendship with the British which included a clause stating that he would oppose the passage of foreign troops through his territories. This agreement, the first Afghan pact with a European power, stipulated joint action in case of Franco-Persian aggression against Afghan or British dominions. Only a few weeks after signing the agreement, Shuja was deposed by his predecessor, Mahmud, whose second reign lasted nine years, until 1818. Mahmud alienated the Muhammadzai, especially Fateh Khan, the son of Painda Khan, who was eventually seized and blinded. Revenge would later be sought and obtained by Fateh Khan's youngest brother, Dost Mohammad.

From 1818 until Dost Mohammad's ascendancy in 1826, chaos reigned in the domains of Ahmad Shah Durrani's empire as various sons of Painda Khan struggled for supremacy. Afghanistan ceased to exist as a single nation, disintegrating for a brief time into a fragmented collection of small units, each ruled by a different Durrani leader.

THE GREAT GAME

The Rise of Dost Mohammad

It was not until 1826 that the energetic Dost Mohammad was able to exert sufficient control over his brothers to take over the throne in Kabul, where he proclaimed himself *amir*. Although the British had begun to show interest in Afghanistan as early as their 1809 treaty with Shuja, it was not until the reign of Dost Mohammad, first of the Muhammadzai rulers, that the opening gambits were played in what came to be known as the "Great Game." The Great Game set in motion the confrontation of the British and Russian empires--whose spheres of influence moved steadily closer to one another until they met in Afghanistan. It also involved Britain's repeated attempts to impose a puppet government in Kabul. The remainder of the nineteenth century saw greater European involvement in Afghanistan and her surrounding territories and heightened conflict among the ambitious local rulers as Afghanistan's fate played out globally.

Dost Mohammad achieved prominence among his brothers through clever use of the support of his mother's Qizilbash tribesmen and his own youthful apprenticeship under his brother, Fateh Khan. Among the many problems he faced was repelling Sikh encroachment on the Pashtun areas east of the Khyber Pass. After working assiduously to establish control and stability in his domains around Kabul, the amir next chose to confront the Sikhs.

In 1834 Dost Mohammad defeated an invasion by the former ruler, Shah Shuja, but his absence from Kabul gave the Sikhs the opportunity to expand westward. Ranjit Singh's forces occupied Peshawar, moving from there into territory ruled directly by Kabul. In 1836 Dost Mohammad's forces, under the command of his son Akbar Khan, defeated the Sikhs at Jamrud, a post fifteen kilometers west of Peshawar. The Afghan leader did not follow up this triumph by retaking Peshawar, however, but instead contacted

Lord Auckland, the new British governor general in India, for help in dealing with the Sikhs. With this letter, Dost Mohammad formally set the stage for British intervention in Afghanistan. At the heart of the Great Game lay the willingness of Britain and Russia to subdue, subvert, or subjugate the small independent states that lay between them.

The debacle of the Afghan civil war left a vacuum in the Hindu Kush area that concerned the British, who were well aware of the many times in history it had been employed as the invasion route to India. In the early decades of the nineteenth century, it became clear to the British that the major threat to their interests in India would not come from the fragmented Afghan empire, the Iranians, or the French, but from the Russians, who had already begun a steady advance southward from the Caucasus.

At the same time, the Russians feared permanent British occupation in Central Asia as the British encroached northward, taking the Punjab, Sindh, and Kashmir. The British viewed Russia's absorption of the Caucasus, the Kirghiz and Turkmen lands, and the Khanates of Khiva and Bukhara with equal suspicion as a threat to their interests in the Indian subcontinent.

In addition to this rivalry between Britain and Russia, there were two specific reasons for British concern over Russia's intentions. First was the Russian influence at the Iranian court, which prompted the Russians to support Iran in its attempt to take Herat, historically the western gateway to Afghanistan and northern India. In 1837 Iran advanced on Herat with the support and advice of Russian officers. The second immediate reason was the presence in Kabul in 1837 of a Russian agent, Captain P. Vitkevich, who was ostensibly there, as was the British agent Alexander Burnes, for commercial discussions.

The British demanded that Dost Mohammad sever all contact with the Iranians and Russians, remove Vitkevich from Kabul, surrender all claims to Peshawar, and respect Peshawar's independence as well as that of Qandahar, which was under the control of his brothers at the time. In return, the British government intimated that it would ask Ranjit Singh to reconcile with the Afghans. When Auckland refused to put the agreement in writing, Dost Mohammad turned his back on the British and began negotiations with Vitkevich.

In 1838 Auckland, Ranjit Singh, and Shuja signed an agreement stating that Shuja would regain control of Kabul and Qandahar with the help of the British and Sikhs; he would accept Sikh rule of the former Afghan provinces already controlled by Ranjit Singh, and that Herat would remain independent. In practice, the plan replaced Dost Mohammad with a British figurehead whose autonomy would be as limited as that of other Indian princes.

It soon became apparent to the British that Sikh participation--advancing toward Kabul through the Khyber Pass while Shuja and the British advanced through Qandahar--would not be forthcoming. Auckland's plan in the spring of 1838 was for the Sikhs--with British support--to place Shuja on the Afghan throne. By summer's end, however, the plan had changed; now the British alone would impose the pliant Shuja.

The First Anglo-Afghan War

To justify his plan, Auckland issued the Simla Manifesto in October 1838, setting forth the necessary reasons for British intervention in Afghanistan. The manifesto stated that in order to insure the welfare of India, the British must have a trustworthy ally on India's western frontier. The British pretense that their troops were merely supporting Shuja's small army in retaking what was once his throne fooled no one. Although the Simla Manifesto stated that British troops would be withdrawn as soon as Shuja was installed in Kabul, Shuja's rule depended entirely on British arms to suppress rebellion and on British funds to buy the support of tribal chiefs. The British denied that they were invading Afghanistan, instead claiming they were merely supporting its legitimate Shuja government "against foreign interference and factious opposition."

From the British point of view, the First Anglo-Afghan War (1838-42) (often called "Auckland's Folly") was an unmitigated disaster, despite the ease with which Dost Mohammad was deposed and Shuja enthroned. An army of British and Indian troops set out from the Punjab in December 1838 and reached Quetta by late March 1839. A month later, the British took Qandahar without a battle. In July, after a two-month delay in Qandahar, the British attacked the fortress of Ghazni, overlooking a plain leading to India, and achieved a decisive victory over Dost Mohammad's troops led by one of his sons. Dost Mohammad fled with his loyal followers across the passes to Bamian, and ultimately to Bukhara. In August 1839, after almost thirty years, Shuja was again enthroned in Kabul. Some British troops returned to India, but it soon became clear that Shuja's rule could only be maintained with the presence of British forces. After he unsuccessfully attacked the British and their Afghan protégé, Dost Mohammad surrendered to them and was exiled in India in late 1840.

By October 1841, however, disaffected Afghan tribes were flocking to support Dost Mohammad's son, Mohammad Akbar, in

Bamian. On January 1, 1842, their presence no longer wanted, an agreement was reached that provided for the safe exodus of the British garrison and its dependents from Afghanistan. Five days later, the retreat began, and as they struggled through the snowbound passes, the British were attacked by Ghilzai warriors. Although Dr. W. Brydon is frequently mentioned as the only survivor of the march to Jalalabad--out of a column of more than 16,000 (consisting of about 4,500 military personnel, both British and Indian, along with as many as 12,000 camp followers) who undertook the retreat--a few more survived as prisoners and hostages. His British protectors gone, Shuja remained in power only a few months before being assassinated in April 1842.

The complete destruction of the garrison prompted brutal retaliation by the British against the Afghans and touched off yet another power struggle for dominance of Afghanistan. In the fall of 1842, British forces from Qandahar and Peshawar entered Kabul just long enough to rescue the few British prisoners and burn the Great Bazaar. Although the foreign invasion provided the Afghan tribes with a temporary sense of unity they had previously lacked, the loss of life and property was followed by a bitter resentment of foreign influence.

The Russians advanced steadily southward toward Afghanistan in the three decades after the First Anglo-Afghan War. In 1842 the Russian border was on the other side of the Aral Sea from Afghanistan, but five short years later the tsar's outposts had moved to the lower reaches of the Amu Darya. By 1865 Tashkent had been formally annexed, as was Samarkand three years later. A peace treaty in 1868 with Amir Muzaffar al-Din, the ruler of Bukhara, virtually stripped him of his independence. Russian control now extended as far as the northern bank of the Amu Darya.

The Second Anglo-Afghan War

After months of chaos in Kabul, Mohammad Akbar secured local control and in April 1843 his father, Dost Mohammad, returned to the throne in Afghanistan. During the Second Anglo-Sikh War (1848-49), his last effort to take Peshawar failed.

By 1854 the British wanted to resume relations with Dost Mohammad, whom they had essentially ignored in the intervening twelve years. The 1855 Treaty of Peshawar reopened diplomatic relations, proclaimed respect for each side's territorial integrity, and pledged both sides as friends of each other's friends and enemies of each other's enemies.

In 1857 an addendum to the 1855 treaty permitted a British military mission to become a presence in Qandahar (but not to Kabul) during a conflict with the Iranians, who had attacked Herat in 1856. In 1863 Dost Mohammad retook Herat with British acquiescence. A few months later, Dost Mohammad died. Sher Ali, his third son, and proclaimed successor, failed to recapture Kabul from his older brother, Mohammad Afzal (whose troops were led by his son, Abdur Rahman) until 1868, after which Abdur Rahman retreated across the Amu Darya and bided his time.

In the years immediately following the First Anglo-Afghan War, and especially after the 1857 uprising against the British (known as the Sepoy Rebellion) in India, Liberal Party governments in London took a political view of Afghanistan as a buffer state. By the time Sher Ali had established control in Kabul in 1868, he found the British ready to support his regime with arms and funds, but nothing more. From then on, relations between the Afghan ruler and Britain deteriorated steadily over the next ten years. The Afghan ruler was worried about the southward encroachment of Russia, which by 1873 had taken over the lands of the khan, or ruler, of Khiva. Sher Ali sent an envoy seeking British advice and support. The previous year, however, the British had signed an agreement with the Russians in which the latter agreed to respect the northern boundaries of Afghanistan and to view the territories of the Afghan amir as outside their sphere of influence. The British, however, refused to give any assurances to the disappointed Sher Ali.

After tension between Russia and Britain in Europe ended with the June 1878 Congress of Berlin, Russia turned its attention to Central Asia. That same summer, Russia sent an uninvited diplomatic mission to Kabul. Sher Ali tried, but failed, to keep them out. Russian envoys arrived in Kabul on July 22, 1878 and on August 14, the British demanded that Sher Ali accept their mission.

The amir not only refused to receive a British mission but threatened to stop it if it were dispatched. Lord Lytton, the viceroy, called Sher Ali's bluff and ordered a diplomatic mission to set out for Kabul on November 21, 1878. The mission was turned back as it approached the eastern entrance of the Khyber Pass, thus triggering the Second Anglo-Afghan War. A British force of about 40,000 fighting men were distributed into military columns which penetrated Afghanistan at three different points. An alarmed Sher Ali attempted to appeal in person to the tsar for assistance, but unable to do so, he returned to Mazar-e-Sharif, where he died the following February.

With British forces occupying much of the country, Sher Ali's son and successor, Yaqub, signed the Treaty of Gandamak in May 1879 to prevent a British invasion of the rest of the country. According to this agreement and in return for an annual subsidy and vague assurances of assistance in case of foreign aggression, Yaqub relinquished control of Afghan foreign affairs to the British. British representatives were installed in Kabul and other locations, British control was extended to the Khyber and Michni passes, and the Afghanistan ceded various frontier areas to Britain. An Afghan uprising opposed to the Treaty of Gandamak was foiled in October 1879. A noted historian, W. Kerr Fraser-Tytler, suggests that Yaqub abdicated because he did not wish to suffer the same fate that befell Shah Shuja following the first war.

ABDUR RAHMAN KHAN, "THE IRON AMIR," 1880-1901

Consolidation of the Modern State

As far as British interests were concerned, Abdur Rahman answered their prayers: a forceful, intelligent leader capable of welding his divided people into a state; and he was willing to accept limitations to his power imposed by British control of his country's foreign affairs and the British buffer state policy. His twenty-one-year reign was marked by efforts to modernize and establish control of the kingdom, whose boundaries were delineated by the two empires bordering it. Abdur Rahman turned his considerable energies to what evolved into the creation of the modern state of Afghanistan.

He achieved this consolidation of Afghanistan in three ways. He suppressed various rebellions and followed up his victories with harsh punishment, execution, and deportation. He broke the stronghold of Pashtun tribes by forcibly transplanting them. He transplanted his most powerful Pashtun enemies, the Ghilzai, and other tribes from southern and south-central Afghanistan to areas north of the Hindu Kush with predominantly non-Pashtun populations. Finally, he created a system of provincial governorates different from old tribal boundaries. Provincial governors had a great deal of power in local matters, and an army was placed at their disposal to enforce tax collection and suppress dissent. Abdur Rahman kept a close eye on these governors, however, by creating an effective intelligence system. During his reign, tribal organization began to erode as provincial government officials allowed land to change hands outside the traditional clan and tribal limits.

Modernization and Development of Institutions

In addition to forging a nation from the splintered regions comprising Afghanistan, Abdur Rahman tried to modernize his kingdom by forging a regular army and the first institutionalized bureaucracy. Despite his distinctly authoritarian personality, Abdur Rahman called for a loya jirgah (*jirgah*--see Glossary), an assemblage of royal princes, important notables, and religious leaders. According to his autobiography, Abdur Rahman had three goals: subjugating the tribes, extending government control through a strong, visible army, and reinforcing the power of the ruler and the royal family.

Abdur Rahman also paid attention to technological advancement. He brought foreign physicians, engineers (especially for mining), geologists, and printers to Afghanistan. He imported European machinery and encouraged the establishment of small factories to manufacture soap, candles, and leather goods. He sought European technical advice on communications, transport, and irrigation. Nonetheless, despite these sweeping internal policies, Abdur Rahman's foreign policy was completely in foreign hands.

The first important frontier dispute was the Panjdeh crisis of 1885, precipitated by Russian encroachment into Central Asia. Having seized the Merv (now Mary) Oasis by 1884, Russian forces were directly adjacent to Afghanistan. Claims to the Panjdeh Oasis were in debate, with the Russians keen to take over all the region's Turkoman domains. After battling Afghan forces in the spring of 1885, the Russians seized the oasis. Russian and British troops were quickly alerted, but the two powers reached a compromise; Russia was in possession of the oasis, and Britain believed it could keep the Russians from advancing any farther. Without an Afghan say in the matter, the Joint Anglo-Russian Boundary Commission agreed the Russians would relinquish the farthest territory captured in their advance but retain Panjdeh. This agreement on these border sections delineated for Afghanistan a permanent northern frontier at the Amu Darya but also the loss of much territory, especially around Panjdeh.

The second section of Afghan border demarcated during Abdur Rahman's reign was in the Wakhan Corridor. The British insisted Abdur Rahman accept sovereignty over this remote region where unruly Kirghiz held sway, he had no choice but to accept Britain's compromise. In 1895 and 1896 another Joint Anglo-Russian Boundary Commission agreed on the frontier boundary to the far northeast of Afghanistan, which bordered Chinese territory (although the Chinese did not formally accept this as on a boundary between the two countries until 1964.)

For Abdur Rahman, delineating the boundary with India (through the Pashtun area) was far more significant, and it was during his reign that the Durand Line was drawn. Under pressure, Abdur Rahman agreed in 1893 to accept a mission headed by the British Indian foreign secretary, Sir Mortimer Durand, to define the limits of British and Afghan control in the Pashtun territories. Boundary limits were agreed on by Durand and Abdur Rahman before the end of 1893, but there is some question about the degree to which Abdur Rahman willingly ceded certain regions. There were indications that he regarded the Durand Line as a delimitation of separate areas of political responsibility, not a permanent international frontier, and that he did not explicitly cede control over certain parts (such as Kurram and Chitral) that were already in British control under the Treaty of Gandamak.

The Durand Line cut through both tribes and villages and bore little relation to the realities of topography, demography, or even military strategy. The line laid the foundation, not for peace between the border regions, but for heated disagreement between the governments of Afghanistan and British India, and later, Afghanistan and Pakistan.

The clearest manifestation that Abdur Rahman's had established control in Afghanistan was the peaceful successor of his eldest son, Habibullah, to the throne on his father's death in October 1901. Although Abdur Rahman had fathered many children, he groomed

Habibullah to succeed him, and he made it difficult for his other sons to contest the succession by keeping power from them and sequestering them in Kabul under his control.

[RESERVED]

THE REIGN OF KING HABIBULLAH, 1901-1919

Habibullah, Abdur Rahman's eldest son but child of a slave mother, kept a close watch on the palace intrigues revolving around his father's more distinguished wife (a granddaughter of Dost Mohammad), who sought the throne for her own son. Although made secure in his position as ruler by virtue of support from the army which was created by his father, Habibullah was not as domineering as Abdur Rahman. Consequently, the influence of religious leaders as well as that of Mahmoud Beg Tarzi, a cousin of the king, increased during his reign. Tarzi, a highly educated, well-traveled poet and journalist, founded an Afghan nationalist newspaper with Abdur Rahman's agreement, and until 1919 he used the newspaper as a platform for rebutting clerical criticism of Western-influenced changes in government and society, for espousing full Afghan independence, and for other reforms. Tarzi's passionate Afghan nationalism influenced a future generation of Asian reformers.

The boundary with Iran was firmly delineated in 1904, replacing the ambiguous line made by a British commission in 1872. Agreement could not be reached, however, on sharing the waters of the Helmand River.

Like all foreign policy developments of this period affecting Afghanistan, the conclusion of the "Great Game" between Russia and Britain occurred without the Afghan ruler's participation. The 1907 Anglo-Russian Convention (Entente) not only divided the region into separate areas of Russian and British influence but also established foundations for Afghan neutrality. The convention provided for Russian acquiescence that Afghanistan was now outside this sphere of influence, and for Russia to consult directly with Britain on matters relating to Russian-Afghan relations. Britain, for its part, would not occupy or annex Afghan territory, or interfere in Afghanistan's internal affairs.

During World War I, Afghanistan remained neutral despite pressure to support Turkey when its sultan proclaimed his nation's participation in what it considered a holy war. Habibullah did, however, entertain a Turco-German mission in Kabul in 1915. After much procrastination, he won an agreement from the Central Powers for a huge payment and arms provision in exchange for attacking British India. But the crafty Afghan ruler clearly viewed the war as an opportunity to play one side off against the other, for he also offered the British to resist a Central Powers from an attack on India in exchange for an end to British control of Afghan foreign policy.

[RESERVED]

THE REIGN OF KING AMANULLAH, 1919-29

On February 20, 1919, Habibullah was assassinated on a hunting trip. He had not declared a succession, but left his third son, Amanullah, in charge in Kabul. Because Amanullah controlled both the national treasury and the army, he was well situated to seize power. Army support allowed Amanullah to suppress other claims and imprison those relatives who would not swear loyalty to him. Within a few months, the new amir had gained the allegiance of most tribal leaders and established control over the cities.

Third Anglo-Afghan War and Independence

Amanullah's ten years of reign initiated a period of dramatic change in Afghanistan in both foreign and domestic politics. Starting in May 1919 when he won complete independence in the month-long Third Anglo-Afghan War with Britain, Amanullah altered foreign policy in his new relations with external powers and transformed domestic politics with his social, political, and economic reforms. Although his reign ended abruptly, he achieved some notable successes, and his efforts failed as much due to the centripetal forces of tribal Afghanistan and the machinations of Russia and Britain as to any political folly on his part.

Amanullah came to power just as the entente between Russia and Britain broke down following the Russian Revolution of 1917. Once again Afghanistan provided a stage on which the great powers played out their schemes against one another. Amanullah attacked the British in May 1919 in two thrusts, taking them by surprise. Afghan forces achieved success in the early days of the war as Pashtun tribesmen on both sides of the border joined forces with them.

The military skirmishes soon ended in a stalemate as the British recovered from their initial surprise. Britain virtually dictated the terms of the 1919 Rawalpindi Agreement, a temporary armistice that provided, somewhat ambiguously, for Afghan self-determination in foreign affairs. Before final negotiations were concluded in 1921, however, Afghanistan had already begun to establish its own foreign policy, including diplomatic relations with the new government in the Soviet Union in 1919. During the 1920s, Afghanistan established diplomatic relations with most major countries, and Amanullah became king in 1923.

The second round of Anglo-Afghan negotiations for final peace were inconclusive. Both sides were prepared to agree on Afghan independence in foreign affairs, as provided for in the previous agreement. The two nations disagreed, however, on the issue that had plagued Anglo-Afghan relations for decades and would continue to cause friction for many more--authority over Pashtun tribes on both sides of the Durand Line. The British refused to concede Afghan control over the tribes on the British side of the line while the Afghans insisted on it. The Afghans regarded the 1921 agreement as only an informal one.

The rivalry of the great powers in the region might have remained subdued had it not been for the dramatic change in government in Moscow brought about by the Bolshevik Revolution of 1917. In their efforts to placate Muslims within their borders, the new Soviet leaders were eager to establish cordial relations with neighboring Muslim states. In the case of Afghanistan, the Soviets could achieve a dual purpose: by strengthening relations with the leadership in Kabul, they could also threaten Britain, which was one of the Western states supporting counterrevolution in the Soviet Union. In his attempts to unclench British control of Afghan foreign policy, Amanullah sent an emissary to Moscow in 1919; Lenin received the envoy warmly and responded by sending a Soviet representative to Kabul to offer aid to Amanullah's government.

Throughout Amanullah's reign, Soviet-Afghan relations fluctuated according Afghanistan's value to the Soviet leadership at a given time; Afghanistan was either viewed as a tool for dealing with Soviet Muslim minorities or for threatening the British. Whereas the Soviets sought Amanullah's assistance in suppressing anti-Bolshevik elements in Central Asia in return for help against the British, the Afghans were more interested in regaining lands across the Amu Darya lost to Russia in the nineteenth century. Afghan attempts to regain the oases of Merv and Panjdeh were easily subdued by the Soviet Red Army.

In May 1921, the Afghans and the Soviets signed a Treaty of Friendship, Afghanistan's first international agreement since gaining full independence in 1919. The Soviets provided Amanullah with aid in the form of cash, technology, and military equipment. Despite this, Amanullah grew increasingly disillusioned with the Soviets, especially as he witnessed the widening oppression of his fellow Muslims across the border.

Anglo-Afghan relations soured over British fear of an Afghan-Soviet friendship, especially with the introduction of a few Soviet planes into Afghanistan. British unease increased when Amanullah maintained contacts with Indian nationalists and gave them asylum in Kabul, and also when he sought to stir up unrest among the Pashtun tribes across the border. The British responded by refusing to address Amanullah as "Your Majesty," and imposing restrictions on the transit of goods through India.

Reform, Popular Reaction, and Forced Abdication

Amanullah's domestic reforms were no less dramatic than his foreign policy initiatives, but those reforms could not match his achievement of complete, lasting independence. Mahmoud Beg Tarzi, Amanullah's father-in-law, encouraged the monarch's interest in social and political reform but urged that it be gradually built upon the basis of a strong army and central government, as had occurred in Turkey under Kemal Atatürk. Amanullah, however, was unwilling to put off implementing his changes.

Amanullah's reforms touched on many areas of Afghan life. In 1921 he established an air force, albeit with only a few Soviet planes and pilots; Afghan personnel later received training in France, Italy, and Turkey. Although he came to power with army support, Amanullah alienated many army personnel by reducing both their pay and size of the forces and by altering recruiting patterns to prevent tribal leaders from controlling who joined the service. Amanullah's Turkish advisers suggested the king retire the older officers, men who were set in their ways and might resist the formation of a more professional army. Amanullah's minister of war, General Muhammad Nadir Khan, a member of the Musahiban branch of the royal family, opposed these changes, preferring instead to recognize tribal sensitivities. The king rejected Nadir Khan's advice and an anti-Turkish faction took root in the army; in 1924 Nadir Khan left the government to become ambassador to France.

If fully enacted, Amanullah's reforms would have totally transformed Afghanistan. Most of his proposals, however, died with his abdication. His transforming social and educational reforms included: adopting the solar calendar, requiring Western dress in parts of Kabul and elsewhere, discouraging the veiling and seclusion of women, abolishing slavery and forced labor, introducing secular education (for girls as well as boys); adult education classes and educating nomads. His economic reforms included restructuring, reorganizing, and rationalizing the entire tax structure, antismuggling and anticorruption campaigns, a livestock census for taxation purposes, the first budget (in 1922), implementing the metric system (which did not take hold), establishing the Bank-i-Melli (National Bank) in 1928, and introducing the afghani as the new unit of currency in 1923.

The political and judicial reforms Amanuallah proposed were equally radical for the time and included the creation of Afghanistan's first constitution (in 1923), the guarantee of civil rights (first by decree and later constitutionally), national registration and identity cards for the citizenry, the establishment of a legislative assembly, a court system to enforce new secular penal, civil, and commercial codes, prohibition of blood money, and abolition of subsidies and privileges for tribal chiefs and the royal family.

Although *sharia* (Islamic law) was to be the residual source of law, it regained prominence after the Khost rebellion of 1923-24. Religious leaders, who had gained influence under Habibullah, were unhappy with Amanullah's extensive religious reforms.

Conventional wisdom holds that the tribal revolt that overthrew Amanullah grew out of opposition to his reform program, although those people most affected by his reforms were urban dwellers not universally opposed to his policies, rather than the tribes. Nevertheless, the king had managed to alienate religious leaders and army members.

The unraveling began, however, when Shinwari Pashtun tribesmen revolted in Jalalabad in November 1928. When tribal forces advanced on the capital, many of the king's troops deserted. Amanullah faced another threat as well: in addition to the Pashtun tribes, forces led by a Tajik tribesman were moving toward Kabul from the north. In January 1929, Amanullah abdicated the throne to his oldest brother, Inayatullah, who ruled for only three days before escaping into exile in India. Amanullah's efforts to recover power by leading a small, ill-equipped force toward Kabul failed. The deposed king crossed the border into India and went into exile in Italy. He died in Zurich in 1960.

TAJIK RULE, JANUARY-OCTOBER 1929

The man who seized Kabul from Amanullah is usually described by historians as a Tajik bandit. A native of Kala Khan, a village thirty kilometers north of Kabul, the new Afghan ruler dubbed himself Habibullah Khan, but others called him Bacha-i Saqqao (Son of the Water Carrier). His attack on Kabul was shrewdly timed to follow the Shinwari rebellion and the defection of much of the army. Habibullah was probably the first Tajik to rule this region since before the Greeks arrived (although some historians believe the Ghorids of the twelfth century to have been Tajiks).

Little is written of Habibullah Khan's nine-month reign, but most historians agree that he could not have held onto power for very long under any conditions. The powerful Pashtun tribes, including the Ghilzai, who had initially supported him against Amanullah, chafed under rule by a non-Pashtun. When Amanullah's last feeble attempt to regain his throne failed, those next in line were the Musahiban brothers, who were also Muhammadzai Barakzai and whose great-grandfather was an older brother of Dost Mohammad.

The five prominent Musahiban brothers included Nadir Khan, the eldest, who had been Amanullah's former minister of war. They were permitted to cross through the North-West Frontier Province (NWFP) to enter Afghanistan and take up arms. Once on the other side, however, they were not allowed back and forth across the border to use British territory as a sanctuary, nor were they allowed to gather together a tribal army on the British side of the Durand Line. However, the Musahiban brothers and the tribes successfully ignored these restrictions.

After several unsuccessful attempts, Nadir and his brothers finally raised a sufficiently large force--mostly from the British side of the Durand Line--to take Kabul on October 10, 1929. Six days later, Nadir Shah, the eldest of the Musahiban brothers, was proclaimed monarch. Habibullah fled Kabul, was captured in Kohistan, and executed on November 3, 1929.

[RESERVED]

MUHAMMAD NADIR SHAH, 1929-33

The new ruler quickly abolished most of Amanullah's reforms, but despite his efforts to rebuild an army that had just been engaged in suppressing a rebellion, the forces remained weak while the religious and tribal leaders grew strong. In 1930, there were uprisings by the Shinwari Pushtuns as well as by another Tajik leader. The same year, a Soviet force crossed the border in pursuit of an Uzbek leader whose forces had been harassing the Soviets from his sanctuary in Afghanistan. He was driven back to the Soviet side by the Afghan army in April 1930, and by the end of 1931 most uprisings had been subdued.

Nadir Shah named a ten-member cabinet, consisting mostly of members of his family, and in September 1930 he called into session a loya jirgah of 286 which confirmed his accession to the throne. In 1931 the king promulgated a new constitution. Despite its appearance as a constitutional monarchy, the document officially instituted a royal oligarchy, and popular participation was merely an illusion.

Although Nadir Shah placated religious factions with a constitutional emphasis on orthodox denominational principles, he also took steps to modernize Afghanistan in material ways, although far less obtrusively than his cousin Amanullah. He improved road construction, especially the Great North Road through the Hindu Kush, and methods of communication. He forged commercial links with the same foreign powers that Amanullah had established diplomatic relations with in the 1920s, and, under the leadership of several prominent entrepreneurs, he initiated a banking system and long-range economic planning. Although his efforts to improve the army did not bear fruit immediately, by the time of his death in 1933 Nadir Shah had created a 40,000-strong force from almost no national army at all. It is notable that Afghanistan's regeneration was carried out with no external assistance whatsoever.

Nadir Shah's brief four year reign ended violently, but he nevertheless accomplished a feat of which his great-great-uncle, Dost Mohammad, would have been proud: he reunited a fragmented Afghanistan. Nadir Shah was assassinated in 1933 by a young man whose family had been feuding with the king since his accession to power.

[RESERVED]

MOHAMMAD ZAHIR SHAH, 1933-73

Zahir Shah, Nadir Shan's son and successor, became Afghanistan's final king. For his first thirty years on the throne, he accepted the tutelage of powerful advisers in the royal family, first his uncles, later his cousin, Mohammad Daoud Khan. And only in the last decade of his sovereignty did Zahir Shah rule as well as reign unencumbered.

Zahir Shah and His Uncles, 1933-53

Three of the four Musahiban brothers survived Nadir Shah's death, and went on to exercise decisive influence over decision making during Zahir Shah's first twenty years of reign. The eldest, Muhammad Hashim, who had been prime minister under the previous king, retained that post until replaced by his youngest brother, Shah Mahmud in 1946.

Hashim put into effect the policies already orchestrated by his brothers. Internal objectives of the new Afghan government focused on strengthening the army and shoring up the economy, including transport and communications. Both goals required foreign assistance. Preferring not to involve the Soviet Union or Britain, Hashim turned to Germany. By 1935 German experts and businessmen had set up factories and hydroelectric projects at the invitation of the Afghan government. Smaller amounts of aid were also forthcoming from Japan and Italy.

Afghanistan joined the League of Nations in 1934, the same year the United States officially recognized Afghanistan. The conclusion of the Treaty of Saadabad with Iran, Iraq, and Turkey in 1937 reinforced Afghanistan's regional ties to neighboring Islamic States.

After the outbreak of World War II, the king proclaimed Afghan neutrality on August 17, 1940, but the Allies were unhappy with the presence of a large group of German nondiplomatic personnel. In October British and Soviet governments demanded that Afghanistan expel all nondiplomatic personnel from the Axis nations. Although the Afghan government considered this demand insulting and illegitimate, it appeared to heed the example of Iran; Britain and the Soviet Union occupied Iran in August 1941 after the government ignored a similar demand. Afghanistan ordered nondiplomatic personnel from all belligerents to leave, and a loya jirgah called by the king supported his policy of absolute neutrality. As the war progressed, it provided larger markets for Afghan agricultural produce (especially in India).

Shortly before the end of the war, Shah Mahmud replaced his older brother as prime minister, ushering in a period of great change in both internal and external policies. Among other things, he presided over the inauguration of the Helmand Valley Project, a cooperative irrigation venture drawing Afghanistan into a closer relationship with the United States, which financed much of the work, He also oversaw the opening of relations with the newly created state of Pakistan, which inherited the Pashtuns from the formerly British-ruled side of the Durand Line. The Pashtuns (or Pakhtuns) sought an independent or semi-independent statehood, that would include the Pashto (or Pakhtu) speakers within Pakistan. This issue would have a resounding impact on Afghan politics, as would Shah Mahmud's political liberalization of the country.

The Pashtunistan Issue

Amir Abdur Rahman had bitterly resented the Durand Line and none of his successors relinquished the notion of Pashtun unity even as they cooperated with the British government on other matters. Eventually, the line dividing the Pashtun people became extremely contentious to the governments of both Afghanistan and Pakistan.

Although the issue became most vexing during partition, British policy in the area before 1947 also aggravated the Pashtunistan problem. In 1901 the British had created a new administrative area, the North-West Frontier Province, which they detached from the Punjab. This new province was divided into Settled Districts and Tribal Agencies, with the latter ruled by a British political agent who reported directly to Delhi.

In 1934 Britain extended self-government to the North-West Frontier Province. By this time, the Indian National Congress (Congress Party), which many Muslims saw as a predominately Hindu organization, had expanded its political activities to include the province. The links between the political leaders of the North-West Frontier Province and the Hindu leaders of Congress were such that a majority in the North-West Frontier Province assembly originally voted to go with India in the partition, a decision which probably would have been rejected by the voting majority in the province. In July 1947, the British held a referendum in the Settled Districts of the province offering the population the choice of either joining an independent India or a now-inevitable Pakistan. An estimated 56 percent of the eligible voters participated and over 90 percent elected to join Pakistan. A loya jirgah was held in the Tribal Agencies. Offered a choice between joining India or Pakistan, the tribes declared their preference for the latter.

Although both Afghanistan and Pakistan made conciliatory gestures, the matter remained unresolved. In one of the government's attempts to suppress tribal uprisings in 1949, a

Pakistani air force plane bombed a village just across the frontier. In response, the Afghan government called a loya jirgah, which promptly declared that it recognized "neither the imaginary Durand nor any similar line" and that all agreements--from the 1893 Durand agreement onward--pertaining to the issue were void. Irregular forces led by a local Pashtun leader crossed the border in 1950 and 1951 to back Afghan claims. Pakistan's government refused to accept the Afghan assertion that it had no control over these men, and both nations' ambassadors were withdrawn, but were exchanged again a few months later.

The issue of an international boundary through Pashtun areas was of great importance to policymakers in Kabul. Pakistan halted vital transshipments of petroleum to Afghanistan for about three months in 1950, presumably in retaliation for Afghan tribal attacks across the border. At this time, Afghan government interest shifted to offers of aid from the Soviet Union and in July 1950 it signed a major agreement with the Soviet Union.

Early Links with the Soviet Union

Pakistan's petroleum cutoff over the Pashtunistan issue and the resulting trade agreement between Afghanistan and the Soviet Union were major watersheds in bilateral relations. The agreement was much more than a barter arrangement exchanging Soviet oil, textiles, and manufactured goods for Afghan wool and cotton; the Soviets offered construction aid to erect petroleum storage facilities, to explore oil and gas reserves in northern Afghanistan, and permission for free transportation of goods across Soviet territory. This new relationship was attractive not only because it made it difficult for Pakistan to disrupt the Afghan economy by blockading or slowing down transshipped goods but also because it provided a balance to United States aid in the Helmand Valley Project. After 1950 Soviet-Afghan trade increased sharply as Soviet technicians were welcomed and a trade office was opened.

Experiment with Liberalized Politics

The third major policy focus of the immediate post-World War II period was Shah Mahmud's experiment in greater political tolerance and liberalization. Encouraged by young, Western-educated members of the political elite, the prime minister allowed National Assembly elections that were distinctly less controlled than they had been in the past; the result was the "liberal parliament" of 1949. He tolerated the activity of opposition political groups. The most vocal of these groups was the Wikh-i-Zalmayan (Awakened Youth), a movement comprised of diverse dissident groups founded in Qandahar in 1947. A newly formed student union not only provided a forum for political debate but also produced theatrical plays critical of Islam and the monarchy. Newspapers criticized the government, and many groups began demanding a more open political system.

But the liberalization went farther than the prime minister had intended. He reacted by attempting to form a government party, and when this failed, he began cracking down. The Kabul University student union was dissolved in 1951; newspapers criticizing the government were closed down; many opposition leaders were jailed. The parliament that was elected in 1952 was a significant step backward from the one that had been elected in 1949. The brief experiment in open politics was over.

Despite its failure, the liberal experiment had important repercussions for the nation's political future: it provided a breeding ground for the revolutionary movement that would come to power in 1978. Future Marxist leaders of Afghanistan, Nur Muhammad Taraki, Babrak Karmal, and Hafizullah Amin were all involved. The government crackdown in 1951 and 1952 that brought an abrupt end to liberalization alienated many young, reformist Afghans who had originally hoped only to improve the existing structure rather than radically transforming it.

Daoud as Prime Minister, 1953-63

In the wake of the failed political reforms of the 1949-52 period came a major shake-up in the royal family. By mid-1953, the younger members of the royal family, which may have included the king himself, challenged domination by the king's uncles. The rift became public in September 1953 when the king's cousin and brother-in-law, Mohammad Daoud, became prime minister. Daoud was the first of the young, Western-educated generation of the royal family to wield power in Kabul. If opponents of the liberal experiment hoped he would move toward a more open political system, however, they were soon disappointed.

Despite Daoud's concern with correcting what he perceived as previous governments' pro-Western bias, his keen interest in modernization manifested itself in continued support of the Helmand Valley Project. Daoud also proceeded cautiously on the question of the emancipation of women. At the fortieth celebration of national independence in 1959, the wives of his ministers appeared unveiled in public at his behest. When religious leaders protested, he challenged them to cite a single verse of the Quran specifically mandating veiling. When they continued to resist, he jailed them for a week.

Daoud's social and economic policies were cautiously reformist and relatively successful. Although fruitful in some respects, his foreign policy caused severe economic dislocation, and, ultimately, his own political eclipse. Daoud's foreign policy was guided by two principles: balancing what he saw as pro-Western orientation on the part of previous governments by improving relations with the Soviet Union (without sacrificing U.S. economic aid), and pursuing the Pashtunistan issue by every possible means. To some extent the two goals were mutually reinforcing when hostile relations with Pakistan caused the Kabul government to fall back on the Soviet Union and its trade and transit link with the rest of the world. Daoud believed that the rivalry between the two superpowers for local allies created a condition whereby he could play one against the other in his search for aid and development assistance.

Daoud's desire for improved bilateral relations with the Soviet Union stepped up a notch to a necessity when the Pakistan-Afghan border was closed for five months in 1955. When the Iranian and United States governments declared that they were unable to create an alternate trade access route through Afghanistan, the Afghans had no choice but to request a renewal of their 1950 transit agreement with the Soviet Union. Ratified in June 1955, it was followed by a new bilateral barter agreement. After the Soviet leaders Nikolay Bulganin and Nikita Khrushchev visited Kabul in 1955, they announced a US$100 million development loan for projects to be mutually agreed upon.

Despite the Cold War climate between the two superpowers, the Daoud regime also sought to strengthen its ties with the United States, whose interest in Afghanistan had grown as a result of United States efforts to forge an alliance among the countries in the "Northern Tier": Afghanistan, Iran, Iraq, Pakistan, and Turkey. Maintaining its nonaligned position, Afghanistan refused to join the United States-sponsored Baghdad Pact. This rebuff did not stop the United States from continuing its low-level aid program, but it was reluctant to provide Afghanistan with military assistance, so Daoud turned to the Soviet Union and its allies for military aid, and in 1955 he received approximately US$25 million of military matériel. In addition, the Soviet bloc also began construction of military airfields in Bagram, Mazar-e-Sharif, and Shindand.

In the face of Daoud's virtual obsession with the Pashtunistan issue, all other foreign policy issues faded in importance. In 1953 and 1954, Daoud applied more of his time-honored techniques to press the Pashunistan issue, such as payments to tribesmen on both sides of the border to subvert the Pakistani government as well as dissemination of hostile propaganda. In 1955, however, the situation became more critical from Daoud's point of view when internal politics forced Pakistan to abolish the four provincial governments of West Pakistan and form one provincial unit (the

One Unit Plan). The Afghan government protested the abolition of the North-West Frontier Province (excluding the Tribal Agencies). The Pakistan border closure in the spring and fall of 1955 again highlighted the need for good relations with the Soviets in order to keep transit routes open for Afghan trade.

Although the Afghans remained unresigned to accepting the status quo on the Pashtunistan issue, the conflict remained dormant for several years (in which time relations improved slightly between the two nations). The 1958 coup that brought General Mohammad Ayub Khan to power in Pakistan also failed to bring on any immediate change in the situation. In 1960 Daoud sent troops across the border into Bajaur in a foolhardy, unsuccessful attempt to manipulate events in that area and to press the Pashtunistan issue, but Afghan military forces were routed by the Pakistan military. During this period the propaganda war, carried on by radio, was relentless.

Afghanistan and Pakistan severed relations on September 6, 1961. Traffic between the two countries came to a halt, just as two of Afghanistan's major export crops, grapes and pomegranates, were ready to be shipped to India. In a valuable public relations gesture, the Soviet Union offered to buy the crops and airlift them from Afghanistan. What the Soviets did not ship, Ariana Afghan Airlines flew to India in 1961 and 1962. At the same time, the United States attempted to mediate the dispute, although its ties with Pakistan were a stumbling block.

In addition, much of the equipment and material provided by foreign aid programs and needed for development projects was held up in Pakistan. Another outgrowth of the dispute was Pakistan's decision to close the border to nomads (members of the Ghilzai, variously known as Powindahs or Suleiman Khel), who had long been spending winters in Pakistan and India and summers in Afghanistan. The Pakistani government statement denying the decision was related to the impasse with Afghanistan appeared disingenuous, and the issue added to the brewing conflict between the two countries. Afghanistan's economic situation continued to deteriorate. The government was heavily dependent upon customs revenues, which fell dramatically; trade suffered; and foreign exchange reserves were seriously depleted.

By 1963 it became clear that neither Daoud of Afghanistan nor Ayub Khan of Pakistan would yield; to settle the issue one of them would have to be removed from power. Despite growing criticism of Ayub among some of his countrymen, his position was generally strong, whereas Afghanistan's economy was suffering. In March 1963, with the backing of the royal family, King Zahir Shah sought Daoud's resignation on the basis that the country's economy was deteriorating as a result of his Pashtunistan policy. Because he controlled the armed forces, Daoud almost certainly had the power to resist the king's request, yet he resigned, and Muhammad Yousuf, a non-Pashtun, German-educated technocrat who had been minister of mines and industries became prime minister.

The King Reigns: The Last Decade of the Monarchy, 1963-73

The new government both represented and sought change. Within two months, ordered an investigation into the abysmal conditions of Afghan prisons, and reached an agreement reestablishing diplomatic and trade relations with Pakistan.

The single greatest achievement of the 1963-73 decade was the promulgation of the 1964 constitution. A mere two weeks after Daoud's resignation, the king appointed a commission to draft a new constitution. In the spring of 1964, he ordered the convening of a loya jirgah--a country-wide gathering that included members of the National Assembly, the Senate, the Supreme Court, and the constitutional commission. One hundred and seventy-six members were elected by the provinces and thirty-four members were appointed directly by the king. Although the assemblage of 452 persons (including six women) that met in September 1964 was composed primarily of officials who could be expected to support the royal line, the loya jirgah also included members elected from around the entire nation. On September 20, the document was signed by the 452 members and ten days later, the kings signature transformed it into the new constitution.

The constitution--and the deliberations that produced it-- demonstrated several noteworthy changes in political thinking. It barred the royal family, other than the king, from participating in politics and government--a provision that was perceived as keeping Daoud out of politics. Individual rights were strongly championed by provincial delegates over tribal ones. Conservative religious members were persuaded to accept provisions they once considered intolerably secular. Although a lengthy debate ensued over whether the word *Afghan* should be used to denote all citizens of Afghanistan (many people regarded it as a reference only to Pashtuns), the loya jirgah agreed that this term should apply to all citizens. The constitution identified Islam as "the sacred religion of Afghanistan," but it was still necessary to persuade many conservative members that their religion had been enshrined in the constitution. Although Article 64 decreed that no law could be enacted that was "repugnant to the basic principles" of Islam, Article 69 defined laws as a resolution passed by the houses of parliament and signed by the king, with *sharia* to be used when no such law existed.

The constitution's provisions for an independent judiciary gave rise to heated debate among religious leaders, many of whom supported the existing legal system based on religion. Although religious judges were incorporated into the new judicial system, the supremacy of secular law was established. The new constitution provided for a constitutional monarchy, with a bicameral legislature, but predominant power remained in the hands of the king.

Most observers described the 1965 elections as remarkably fair. The 216-member Wolesi Jirgah, or the lower house of parliament, included representation not only by antiroyalists but also by the left and right of the political spectrum. Included were supporters of the king, Pashtun nationalists, entrepreneurs and industrialists, political liberals, a small group of leftists, and conservative Muslim leaders still opposed to secularization. The king nominated a new prime minister, Mohammad Hashim Maiwandwal, who quickly established friendly relations with the students, while making it clear that he was in charge and there were limits to student political activity.

On January 1, 1965, the People's Democratic Party of Afghanistan (PDPA) was founded. The PDPA, a communist party in fact if not in name, was established for the primary purpose of gaining parliamentary seats. The PDPA was comprised of a small group of men, followers of Nur Mohammad Taraki and Babrak Karmal, both avowed Marxist-Leninists with a pro-Moscow orientation. The fact that four PDPA members won parliamentary seats suggests that government efforts to prevent the success of its leftist opponents by intervening in the balloting were halfhearted. Taraki, one of the four PDPA members elected to parliament in 1965, started the first major leftist newspaper, *Khalq* (Masses), which lasted little more than a month before being silenced by a government ban.

The Afghan political system remained suspended between democracy and monarchy, although it was, in reality, much closer to the latter. Political parties continued to be prohibited because the king refused to sign legislation allowing them. Democracy nevertheless maintained a toehold in the lower house of parliament where free criticism of government policies and personnel was aired.

In 1967, only a year and a half after its founding, the PDPA had split into several factions. The two most important of these were the Khalq (Masses) faction headed by Taraki and the Parcham (Banner) faction headed by Karmal. Although the split was couched in ideological terms, it was largely due to personality differences between Taraki and Karmal and to their respective preferences in organizing tactics. Taraki favored a Leninist-type party based on the working class, while Karmal wanted a broad democratic front. Supporters of Khalq were primarily Pashtuns

65

from rural Afghanistan, while Parchamis tended to be from urban areas, to come from a better socio-economic background than Khalqis. Unlike the Khalqis, Parchamis included many non-Pashtuns who spoke Dari (Persian) in their ranks.

The monarchy did not treat both factions equally. Karmal's Parcham faction was allowed to publish its own newspaper, *Parcham*, for more than a year (from March 1968 to July 1969) while the Khalq faction had its paper banned. As a result, Khalq accused Parcham of having connections with the king and bitterly denounced its rival as the "Royal Communist Party."

The 1969 parliamentary elections, when voter turnout was not much greater than in 1965 produced a legislative assembly essentially consistent with the real population and distribution of power in the hinterland, in that conservative landowners and businessmen predominated and many more non-Pashtuns were elected than in the previous legislature. Most of the urban liberals and all of the female delegates lost their seats. Few leftists remained in the new parliament, although Karmal and Hafizullah Amin had been elected from districts in and near Kabul. Former prime minister Maiwandwal, a democratic socialist, lost his seat when the government selectively influenced the elections.

Between 1969 and 1973, instability ruled Afghan politics. The parliament was lethargic and deadlocked. Public dissatisfaction over the unstable government prompted growing political polarization as both the left and the right began to attract more members. Still personally popular, the king nevertheless came under increasing criticism for not supporting his own prime ministers.

It was in this atmosphere of internal discontent and polarization and external shakiness that Daoud implemented the coup d'état he had been planning for a year in response to the "anarchy and the anti-national attitude of the regime." While the king was out of the country for medical treatment, Daoud and a small military group seized power in an almost bloodless coup. The stability Zahir Shah had sought through constitutionally sanctioned limited democracy had not been achieved, and was a generally favorable response greeted Daoud's reemergence even though it meant the demise of the monarchy Ahmad Shah Durrani established in 1747.

DAOUD'S REPUBLIC, JULY 1973- APRIL 1978

The welcome Daoud received on returning to power on July 17, 1973 reflected the citizenry's disappointment with the lackluster politics of the preceding decade. King Zahir's "New Democracy" had promised much but had delivered little. Daoud's comeback was a return to traditional strongman rule and he was a particularly appealing figure to military officers. As prime minister, Daoud had obtained large supplies of modern arms from the Soviet Union and he had been a former army officer himself. Also, his strong position on the Pashtunistan issue had not been forgotten by conservative Pashtun officers.

Daoud discussed rebellion for more than a year with various opposition elements--both moderates and leftists, including military officers who were members of both the Khalqi and Parchami factions of the PDPA. Certainly the communists had worked vigorously to undermine Zahir Shah's experiment in constitutional democracy. Their inflammatory speeches in parliament and organized street riots were tactics which alarmed the king to the degree that he refused to sign the law legalizing political parties. Karmal's Parcham faction became integrally involved in planning the coup. There is general agreement that Daoud had been meeting with what he called various "friends" for more than a year. The coup itself was carried out by junior officers trained in the Soviet Union. Some Afghans suspected that Daoud and Karmal had been in touch for many years and that Daoud had used him as an informant on the leftist movement. No strong link can be cited to support this, however, other than the closeness between Karmal's father, an army general, and Daoud. At the time of the July 1973 coup, which took place when the king was in Italy receiving eye treatment at the medicinal mud baths at Ischia, Italy, it was sometimes difficult to assess the factional and party affiliation of the officers who took place. Despite a number of conversions of Parchamis to the Khalqi faction by the time of the communist coup of April 1978 which overthrew Daoud, both party and factional loyalties became obvious after the PDPA took power.

Although leftists had played a central role in the coup, and despite the appointment of two leftists as ministers, evidence suggests that the coup was Daoud's alone. Officers personally loyalto him were placed in key positions while young Parchamis were sent to the provinces, probably to get them out of Kabul, until Daoud had purged the leftist officers by the end of 1975.

The next year, Daoud established his own political party, the National Revolutionary Party, which became the focus of all political activity. In January 1977, a loyal jirgah approved Daoud's constitution establishing a presidential, one party system of government.

Any resistance to the new regime was suppressed. A coup attempt by Maiwandwal, which may have been planned before Daoud took power, was subdued shortly after his coup. In October 1973, Maiwandwal, a former prime minister and a highly respected former diplomat, died in prison at a time when Parchamis controlled the Ministry of Interior under circumstances corroborating the widespread belief that he had been tortured to death.

While both of the PDPA's factions had attempted to collaborate with Daoud before the 1973 coup, Parcham used its advantage to recruit on an unprecedented scale immediately following the coup. Daoud, however, soon made it clear that he was no front man and that he had not adopted the claims of any ideological faction. He began in the first months of his regime to ease Parcharmis out of his cabinet. Perhaps not to alienate the Soviet Union, Daoud was careful to cite inefficiency and not ideological reasons for the dismissals. Khalq, seeing an opportunity to make some short-term gains at Parcham's expense, suggested to Daoud that "honest" Khalqis replace corrupt Parchamis. Daoud, wary of ideologues, ignored this offer.

Daoud's ties with the Soviet Union, like his relations with Afghan communists, deteriorated during his five year presidency. This loosening of ties with the Soviet Union was gradual. Daoud's shift to the right and realignment made the Soviets anxious but western observers noted that Daoud remained solicitous of Soviet interests and Afghanistan's representative in the United Nations voted regularly with the Soviet Bloc or with the group of nonaligned countries. The Soviets remained by far Afghanistan's largest aid donor and were influential enough to insist that no Western activity, economic or otherwise, be permitted in northern Afghanistan.

Daoud still favored a state-centered economy, and, three yearsafter coming to power, he drew up an ambitious seven-year economic plan (1976-83) that included major projects and required a substantial influx of foreign aid. As early as 1974, Daoud began distancing himself from over-reliance on the Soviet Union for military and economic support. That same year, he formed a military training program with India, and opened talks with Iran on economic development aid. Daoud also turned to other oil-rich Muslim nations, such as Saudi Arabia, Iraq, and Kuwait, for financial assistance.

Pashtunistan zealots confidently expected the new president to raise this issue with Pakistan, and in the first few months of the new regime, bilateral relations were poor. Efforts by Iran and the United States to cool a tense situation succeeded after a time, and by 1977 relations between Pakistan and Afghanistan had notably improved. During Daoud's March 1978 visit to Islamabad, an agreement was reached whereby President Mohammad Zia ul-Haq of Pakistan released Pashtun and Baloch militants from prison in exchange for Daoud withdrawing support for these groups and expelling Pashtun and Baloch militants taking refuge in Afghanistan.

Daoud's initial visit to the Soviet Union in 1974 was friendly, despite disagreement on the Pashtunistan issue. By the time of Daoud's second visit in April 1977, the Soviets knew of his purge of the left begun in 1975, his removal of Soviet advisers from some Afghan military units, and his changes in military training whereby other nations, especially India and Egypt, trained Afghans with

Soviet weapons. Despite official goodwill, unofficial reports circulated of sharp Soviet criticism of anticommunists in Daoud's new cabinet, of his failure to cooperate with the PDPA, and of his criticism of Cuba's role in the nonaligned movement. Furthermore, Daoud was friendly with Iran and Saudi Arabia, and he had scheduled a visit to Washington for the spring of 1978.

By 1978 Daoud had achieved little of what he had set out to accomplish. Despite good harvests in 1973 and subsequent years, no real economic progress had been made, and the Afghan standard of living had not improved. By the spring of 1978, he had alienated most key political groups by gathering power into his own hands and refusing to tolerate dissent. Although Muslim fundamentalists had been the object of repression as early as 1974, their numbers had nonetheless increased. Diehard Pashtunistan supporters were disillusioned with Daoud's rapprochement withPakistan, especially by what they regarded as his commitment in the 1977 agreement not to aid Pashtun militants in Pakistan.

Most ominous for Daoud were developments among Afghan communists. In March 1977, despite reaching a fragile agreement on reunification, Parcham and Khalq remained mutually suspicious. The military arms of each faction were not coordinated because, by this time, Khalqi military officers vastly outnumbered Parchami officers and feared the latter might inform Daoud of this, raising his suspicion that a coup was imminent. Although plans for a coup had long been discussed, according to a statement by Hafizullah Amin, the April 1978 coup was implemented about two years ahead of time.

The April 19, 1978, funeral for Mir Akbar Khyber, a prominent Parchami ideologue who had been murdered, served as a rallying point for Afghan communists. An estimated 10,000 to 30,000 persons gathered to hear stirring speeches by Taraki and Karmal. Shocked by this demonstration of communist unity, Daoud ordered the arrest of PDPA leaders, but he reacted too slowly. It took him a week to arrest Taraki, and Amin was merely placed under house arrest. According to later PDPA writings, Amin sent complete orders for the coup from his home while it was under armed guard using his family as messengers. The army had been put on alert on April 26 because of a presumed "anti-Islamic" coup. Given Daoud's repressive and suspicious mood, officers known to have differed with Daoud, even those without PDPA ties or with only tenuous connections to the communists, moved hastily to prevent their own downfall.

On April 27, 1978, a coup d'état beginning with troop movements at the military base at Kabul International Airport, gained ground slowly over the next twenty-four hours as rebels battled units loyal to Daoud in and around the capital. Daoud and most of his family were shot in the presidential palace the following day. Two hundred and thirty-one years of royal rule by Ahmad Shah and his descendants had ended, but it was less clear what kind of regime had succeeded them.

COMMUNISM, REBELLION, AND SOVIET INTERVENTION

The divided PDPA succeeded the Daoud regime with a new government under the leadership of Nur Muhammad Taraki of the Khalq faction. In 1967 the PDPA had split into two groups--Khalq and Parcham--but ten years later, the efforts of the Soviet Union had brought the factions back together, however unstable the merger.

A critical assessment of the period between the Saur (April) Revolution of 1978 and the complete withdrawal of Soviet troops in February 1989 requires analysis of three different, yet closely intertwined, series of events: those within the PDPA government of Afghanistan; those involving the *mujahidin* ("holy warriors") who fought the communist regime in Kabul from bases in Pakistan, Iran, and Afghanistan; and those concerning the Soviet Union's invasion in December 1979 and withdrawal nine years later.

In Kabul, the initial cabinet appeared to be carefully constructed to alternate ranking positions between Khalqis and Parchamis: Taraki was prime minister, Karmal was senior deputy prime minister, and Hafizullah Amin of Khalq was foreign minister. In early July, however, the Khalqi purge of Parchamis began with Karmal dispatched to Czechoslovakia as ambassador (along with others shipped out of the country). Amin appeared to be the principal beneficiary of this strategy, since he now ranked second, behind Taraki. The regime also issued a series of decrees, many of which were viewed by conservatives as opposing Islam, including one declaring the equality of the sexes. Land reform was decreed, as was a prohibition on usury.

Internal rebellion against the regime began in Afghanistan in the summer and fall of 1978. A number of attempts by Parchamis to oust the Khalqis were reported. The intense rivalry between Taraki and Amin within the Khalq faction heated up, culminating in the death--admittedly the murder--of Taraki. In September 1979, Taraki's followers, with Soviet complicity, had made several attempts on Amin's life. The final attempt backfired, however, and it was Taraki who was eliminated and Amin, who assumed power in Afghanistan. The Soviets had at first backed Amin, but they realized that he was too rigidly Marxist-Leninist to survive politically in a country as conservative and religious as Afghanistan.

Taraki's death was first noted in the Kabul Times on 10 October and reported that the former leader only recently hailed as the "great teacher...great genius...great leader" had died quietly "of serious illness, which he had been suffering for some time." Less than three months later, after the Amin government had been overthrown, the newly installed followers of Babrak Karmal gave another account of Taraki's death. According to this account, Amin ordered the commander of the palace guard to have Taraki executed. Taraki reportedly was suffocated with a pillow over his head. Amin's emergence from the power struggle within the small divided communist party in Afghanistan alarmed the Soviet and would usher in the series of events which lead to the Soviet invasion.

During this period, many Afghans fled to Pakistan and Iran and began organizing a resistance movement to the "atheistic" and "infidel" communist regime backed by the Soviets. Although the groups organizing in the Pakistani city of Peshawar would later, after the Soviet invasion, be described by the western press as "freedom fighters"--as if their goal were to establish a representative democracy in Afghanistan--in reality these groups each had agendas of their own that were often far from democratic.

Outside observers usually identify the two warring groups as "fundamentalists" and "traditionalists." Rivalries between these groups continued during the Afghan civil war that followed the Soviet withdrawal. The rivalries of these groups brought the plight of the Afghans to the attention of the West, and it was they who received military assistance from the United States and a number of other nations.

The fundamentalists based their organizing principle around mass politics and included several divisions of the Jamiat-i-Islami. The leader of the parent branch, Burhanuddin Rabbani, began organizing in Kabul before repression of religious conservatives, which began in 1974, forced him to flee to Pakistan during Daoud's regime. Perhaps best known among the leaders was Gulbaddin Hikmatyar, who broke with Rabbani to form another resistance group, the Hizb-e-Islami, which became Pakistan's favored arms recipient. Another split, engineered by Yunus Khales, resulted in a second group using the name Hizb-e-Islami--a group that was somewhat more moderate than Hikmatyar's. A fourth fundamentalist group was the Ittehad-i-Islami led by Rasool Sayyaf. Rabbani's group received its greatest support from northern Afghanistan where the best known resistance commander in Afghanistan--Ahmad Shah Massoud--a Tajik, like Rabbani, operated against the Soviets with considerable success.

The organizing principles of traditionalist groups differed from those of the fundamentalists. Formed from loose ties among *ulama* in Afghanistan, the traditionalist leaders were not concerned, unlike fundamentalists, with redefining Islam in Afghan society but instead focused on the use of the *sharia* as the source of law (interpreting the *sharia* is a principal role of the ulama). Among the three groups in Peshawar, the most important was the Jebh-e-Nejat-e-Milli led by Sibghatullah Mojadeddi. Some of the traditionalists were willing to accept restoration of the monarchy and looked to former King Zahir Shah, exiled in Italy, as the ruler.

Other ties also were important in holding together some resistance groups. Among these were links within *sufi* orders, such as the Mahaz-e-Milli Islami, one of the traditionalist groups associated with the Gilani *sufi* order led by Pir Sayyid Gilani. Another group, the Shia Muslims of Hazarajat, organized the refugees in Iran.

In Kabul, Amin's ascension to the top position was quick. The Soviets had a hand in Taraki's attempts on Amin's life and were not pleased with his rise. Amin began unfinished attempts to moderate what many Afghans viewed as an anti-Islam regime. Promising more religious freedom, repairing mosques, presenting copies of the Koran to religious groups, invoking the name of Allah in his speeches, and declaring that the Saur Revolution was "totally based on the principles of Islam." Yet many Afghans held Amin responsible for the regime's harshest measures and the Soviets, worried about their huge investment in Afghanistan might be jeopardized, increased the number of "advisers" in Afghanistan. Amin become the target of several assassination attempts in early and mid-December 1979.

The Soviets began their invasion of Afghanistan on December 25, 1979. Within two days, they had secured Kabul, deploying a special Soviet assault unit against Darulaman Palace, where elements of the Afghan army loyal to Amin put up a fierce, but brief resistance. With Amin's death at the palace, Babrak Karmal, exiled leader of the Parcham faction of the PDPA was installed by the Soviets as Afghanistan's new head of government.

A number of theories have been advanced for the Soviet action. These interpretations of Soviet motives do not always agree--what is known for certain is that the decision was influenced by many factors--that in Brezhnev's words the decision to invade Afghanistan was truly "was no simple decision." Two factors were certain to have figured heavily in Soviet calculations. The Soviet Union, always interested in establishing a *cordon sanitaire* of subservient or neutral states on its frontiers, was increasingly alarmed at the unstable, unpredictable situation on its southern border. Perhaps as important, the Brezhnev doctrine declared that the Soviet Union had a "right" to come to the assistance of an endangered fellow socialist country. Presumably Afghanistan was a friendly regime that could not survive against growing pressure from the resistance without direct assistance from the Soviet Union.

Whatever the Soviet goals may have been, the international response was sharp and swift. United States President Jimmy Carter, reassessing the strategic situation in his State of the Union address in January, 1980, identified Pakistan as a "front-line state" in the global struggle against communism. He reversed his stand of a year earlier that aid to Pakistan be terminated as a result of its nuclear program and offered Pakistan a military and economic assistance package if it would act as a conduit for United States and other assistance to the *mujahidin*. Pakistani president Zia ul-Haq refused Carter's package but later a larger aid offer from the Reagan administration was accepted. Questions about Pakistan's nuclear program were, for the time being, set aside. Assistance also came from China, Egypt, and Saudi Arabia. Also forth coming was international aid to help Pakistan deal with more than 3 million fleeing Afghan refugees.

The Soviets grossly underestimated the huge cost of the Afghan venture--described, in time, as the Soviet Union's Vietnam--to their state. International opposition also became increasingly vocal. The foreign ministers of the Organization of the Islamic Conference deplored the invasion and demanded Soviet withdrawal at a meeting in Islamabad in January 1980. Action by the United Nations (UN) Security Council was impossible because the Soviets were armed with veto power, but the UN General Assembly regularly passed resolutions opposing the Soviet occupation.

Pakistan proposed talks among the countries directly involved and, although they did not meet, Pakistan and Afghanistan began "proximity" talks in June 1982 through UN official Diego Cordovez. Although these sessions continued for a seemingly interminable length of time--joined by the Soviet Union and the United States--they eventually resulted in an agreement on Soviet withdrawal from Afghanistan.

Other events outside Afghanistan, especially in the Soviet Union, contributed to the eventual agreement. The toll in casualties, economic resources, and loss of support at home increasingly felt in the Soviet Union was causing criticism of the occupation policy. Brezhnev died in 1982, and after two short-lived successors, Mikhail Gorbachev assumed leadership in March 1985. As Gorbachev opened up the country's system, it became more clear that the Soviet Union wished to find a face-saving way to withdraw from Afghanistan.

The civil war in Afghanistan was guerrilla warfare and a war of attrition between the several communist (that is, PDPA) controlled regimes and the *mujahidin*; it cost both sides a great deal. Many Afghans, perhaps as many as five million, or one-quarter of the country's population, fled to Pakistan and Iran where they organized into guerrilla groups to strike Soviet and government forces inside Afghanistan. Others remained in Afghanistan and also formed fighting groups; perhaps most notable was one led by Ahmad Shah Massoud in the northeastern part of Afghanistan. These various groups were supplied with funds to purchase arms, principally from the United States, Saudi Arabia, China, and Egypt. Despite high casualties on both sides, pressure continued to mount on the Soviet Union, especially after the United States brought in Stinger anti-aircraft missiles which severely reduced the effectiveness of Soviet air cover.

The effects of the civil war and Soviet invasion had an impact well beyond Afghanistan's boundaries. Most observers consider Afghanistan a major step along the road to the eventual dissolution of the Soviet Union.

Meanwhile, a change had taken place in Kabul. On May 4, 1986, Karmal resigned as secretary general of the PDPA and was replaced by Najibullah. Karmal retained the presidency for a while, but power had shifted to Najibullah, who had previously headed the State Information Service (Khadamate Ettelaate Dowlati-- KHAD), the Afghan secret service agency. Najibullah tried to diminish differences with the resistance and appeared prepared to allow Islam a greater role as well as legalize opposition groups, but any moves he made toward concessions were rejected out of hand by the *mujahidin*.

Proximity talks in Geneva continued, and on April 14, 1988, Pakistan and Afghanistan reached an agreement providing for the withdrawal of Soviet troops from Afghanistan in nine months, the creation of a neutral Afghan state, and the repatriation of the Afghan refugees. The United States and the Soviet Union would act as guarantors of the agreement. The treaty was less well-received by many *mujahidin* groups who demanded Najibullah's departure as the price for advising their refugee followers to return to Afghanistan.

Nevertheless, the agreement on withdrawal held, and on February 15, 1989, the last Soviet troops departed on schedule from Afghanistan. Their exit, however, did not bring either lasting peace or resettlement, as Afghanistan went from one civil war to another.

* * *

An indispensable book for exploring Afghan history is Louis Dupree's monumental work, *Afghanistan*, which includes a wealth of information from the point of view of a scholar who spent many years in the country. The foremost British history of Afghanistan, W. Kerr Fraser-Tytler's book, *Afghanistan: A Study of Political*

Developments in Central and Southern Asia, written from the perspective of years spent in the region, has valuable insights into all periods of Afghan history but especially the nineteenth century. Arnold Charles Fletcher's *Afghanistan: Highway of Conquest* also provides useful insights. In the twentieth century, more detailed studies of specific subperiods have been recorded. Leon B. Poullada's *Reform and Rebellion in Afghanistan, 1919-1929* is a fascinating and well-written scholarly study of King Amanullah's reign that also includes insights applicable to other periods of Afghan history. (For further information and complete citations, see Bibliography.)

Data as of 1995.

CHAPTER 2. THE SOCIETY
AND ITS ENVIRONMENT

THE HOPE AND EXHILARATION felt among Afghans as the last Soviet troops retreated from their country in early 1989 gave way to frustration within months. Disparate Afghan groups had struggled valiantly against a common enemy, but the extent of the discord and rivalries which characterized their efforts became ominously evident.

Many of those who marveled at the determined and tenacious Afghan response to the invasion of their country have questioned why these same people have turned upon themselves with equal ferocity. Numbers of answers lie in the impact of the Soviet-Afghan War upon Afghan society.

The regional and internal conflicts that erupted after the end of the war are the effects of that war. Islam as a measure of national identity is challenging a century of inroads by secular institutions. Traditional Afghan methods of conflict resolution guided by the spirit of egalitarianism and respect for others are being severely thwarted in an environment surfeited with modern weaponry supplied by outsiders pursuing a multiplicity of regional agendas centered on Afghanistan. Massive drug trafficking created during the war exacerbates the conflict. The persistent rise and fall of individuals forging power from these weapons and drugs fuel self-interests, preclude peace and stretch taut the fabric of the society.

Society in predominately Islamic Afghanistan is defined by a rich melange of variety reflecting its position at the hub of four great cultural zones. Central Asia, China, the Indian subcontinent and the Iranian plateau extend to its borders. Builders of empires, traders and pilgrims as well as those seeking haven from upheavals in their own societies have come to this land throughout the centuries. Some merely passed through; others settled to make it their homeland. Whatever the manner of their arrival, each impressed their own cultural mores on the society.

The Afghan area thus evolved as a zone of cultural transition with a complex ethnolinguistic population as varied as its geography which encompasses fertile mountain valleys in the east, plains and grasslands in the north, a central mountain core, and deserts and semideserts in the west and southwest. The inhabitants of these different areas take pride in these cultural differentiations and follow their own customs, distinct tribal norms, religious variations, divergent attitudes toward family and gender, and contrasting subsistence life-styles.

As the twenty-first century approaches, all Afghans face the challenge of rebuilding their civic society -- a struggle as daunting as their struggle was against the Soviet Union.

THE NATURAL ENVIRONMENT

Afghanistan's rugged terrain and seasonally harsh climate have not deterred foreign invaders who coveted this land or sought to cross it on the road to further conquests. The history of Afghanistan is replete with tales of invasion. Yet the rugged landscape combined with the fiercely independent spirit of the Afghan people have seriously impeded and often repulsed would-be conquerors.

Afghanistan resembles an irregularly shaped hanging leaf with the Wakhan Corridor and the Pamir Knot as its stem in the northeast. Situated between 29 35' and 38 40' north latitude and 60 31' and 75 00' east latitude, it encompasses approximately 652,290 square kilometers, roughly the size of Texas, stretching 1,240 kilometers from east to west and 565 kilometers from north to south. Afghanistan is completely landlocked, bordered by Iran to the west (925 kilometers), by the Central Asian States of Turkmenistan, Uzbekistan, and Tajikistan to the north and northeast (2,380 kilometers), by China at the easternmost top of the Wakhan Corridor (96 kilometers), and by Pakistan to the east and south (2,432 kilometers).

Mountains

Mountains dominate the landscape, forming a terrigenous skeleton, traversing the center of the country, running generally in a northeast-southwest direction. More than 49 percent of the total land area lies above 2,000 meters. Although geographers differ on the division of these mountains into systems, they agree that the Hindukush system, the most important, is the westernmost extension of the Pamir Mountains, the Karakorum Mountains, and the Himalayas.

The origin of the term Hindukush (which translates as Hindu

Killer) is also a point of contention. Three possibilities have been put forward: that the mountains memorialize the Indian slaves who perished in the mountains while being transported to Central Asian slave markets; that the name is merely a corruption of Hindu Koh, the pre-Islamic name of the mountains that divided Hindu southern Afghanistan from non-Hindu northern Afghanistan; or, that the name is a posited Avestan appellation meaning "water mountains."

The mountain peaks in the eastern part of the country reach more than 7,000 meters. The highest of these is Nowshak at 7,485 meters. Mount Everest in Nepal stands 8,796 meters high. The Pamir mountains, which Afghans refer to as the 'Roof of the World," extend into Tajikistan, China and Kashmir.

The mountains of the Hindukush system diminish in height as they stretch westward: toward the middle, near Kabul, they extend from 4,500 to 6,000 meters; in the west, they attain heights of 3,500 to 4,000 meters. The average altitude of the Hindukush is 4,500 meters. The Hindukush system stretches about 966 kilometers laterally, and its median north-south measurement is about 240 kilometers. Only about 600 kilometers of the Hindukush system is called the Hindukush mountains. The rest of the system consists of numerous smaller mountain ranges including the Koh-e Baba; Salang; Koh-e Paghman; Spin Ghar (also called the eastern Safid Koh); Suleiman; Siah Koh; Koh-e Khwaja Mohammad; Selseleh-e Band-e Turkestan. The western Safid Koh, the Siah Band and Doshakh are commonly referred to as the Paropamisus by western scholars.

Numerous high passes (*kotal*) transect the mountains, forming a strategically important network for the transit of caravans. The most important mountain pass is the Kotal-e Salang (3,878 meters); it links Kabul and points south to northern Afghanistan. The completion of a tunnel within this pass in 1964 reduced travel time between Kabul and the north to a few hours. Previously access to the north through the Kotal-e Shibar (3,260 meters) took three days. The Salang Tunnel at 3363 meters and the extensive network of galleries on the approach roads were constructed with

Soviet financial and technological assistance and involved drilling 1.7 miles through the heart of the Hindukush.

Before the Salang road was constructed, the most famous passes in the Western historical perceptions of Afghanistan were those leading to the Indian subcontinent. They include the Khyber Pass (,1027 meters), in Pakistan, and the Kotal-e Lataband (2,499 meters) east of Kabul, which was superseded in 1960 by a road constructed within the Kabul River's most spectacular gorge, the Tang-e Gharu. This remarkable engineering feat completed in 1960 reduced travel time between Kabul and the Pakistan border from two days to a few hours.

The roads through the Salang and Tang-e Gharu passes played critical strategic roles during the recent conflicts and were used extensively by heavy military vehicles. Consequently these roads are in very bad repair. Many bombed out bridges have been repaired, but numbers of the larger structures remain broken. Periodic closures due to conflicts in the area seriously affect the economy and well-being of many regions, for these are major routes carrying commercial trade, emergency relief and reconstruction assistance supplies destined for all parts of the country.

There are a number of other important passes in Afghanistan. Wakhjir (4,923 meters), proceeds from the Wakhan Corridor into Xinjiang, China, and into Kashmir. Passes which join Afghanistan to Chitral, Pakistan, include the Baroghil (3,798 meters) and the Kachin (5,639 meters), which also cross from the Wakhan. Important passes located farther west are the Shotorgardan (3,720 meters), linking Logar and Paktiya provinces; the Bazarak (2,713 meters), leading into Mazar-i-Sharif; the Khawak (3,550 meters)in the Panjsher Valley, and the Anjuman (3,858 meters) at the head of the Panjsher Valley giving entrance to the north. The Hajigak (2,713 meters) and Unai (3,350 meters) lead into the eastern Hazarajat and Bamiyan Valley. The passes of the Paropamisus in the west are relatively low, averaging around 600 meters; the most well-known of these is the Sabzak between Herat and Badghis provinces, which links the western and northwestern parts of Afghanistan.

These mountainous areas are mostly barren, or at the most sparsely sprinkled with trees and stunted bushes. True forests, found mainly in the eastern provinces of Nuristan and Paktiya, cover barely 2.9 of the country's area. Even these small reserves have been disastrously depleted by the war and through illegal exploitation. The forests are in fact in a crisis situation. A 1996 a FAO report estimated that of the 4.7 million acres of forests existing at the beginning of the war, in 1979, considerably less than one million acres survive today.

Rivers

In addition to its mountains, the country possesses many rivers, river basins, lakes and desert areas. The four major river systems are the Amu Darya, the Oxus of antiquity, (boundary with Central Asia, 1,100 kilometers in Afghanistan); the Hilmand (1,300 kilometers); the Harirud (650 kilometers in Afghanistan); and the Kabul (460 kilometers). Only the Kabul River, joining the Indus system in Pakistan, leads to the sea. Many rivers and streams simply empty into arid portions of the country, spending themselves through evaporation without replenishing the four major systems; others flow only seasonally.

Three major dams harness these rivers for land reclamation and hydroelectric purposes: the Arghandab Dam above Kandahar, completed in 1952, is 145-feet-high and 1,740-feet-long and has a storage capacity of 388,000 acre-feet of water; the Kajakai Dam on the Hilmand River, completed in 1953, is 300-feet-high and 887-feet-long, with a storage capacity of 1,495,000 acre-feet of water; the Naglu Dam on the Kabul River west of Jalalabad, completed in the 1960s, is 361-feet-high and 919-feet-long, stores 304,000 acre-feet of water. These large dams were not destroyed by war, but because of lack of maintenance, looted cables and major silting in the reservoirs, none are functioning to full capacity.

Regions

Scholars disagree over the division, number and definitions of Afghanistan's regions. Louis Dupree's geographic paradigm is one of the most respected and is based on the regional division of human geography and ecology. He divides Afghanistan into eleven geographic zones. The first six--the Wakhan Corridor-Pamir Knot, Badakhshan, Central Mountains, Eastern Mountains, Northern Mountains and Foothills, Southern Mountains and Foothills--are connected to the Hindukush systems. The remaining five-- Turkistan Plains, Herat-Farah Lowlands, Sistan Basin-Hilmand Valley, Western Stony Desert, and Southwestern Sandy Desert-- comprise deserts and plains "which surround the Mountains in the north, west and southwest." Medieval geographies speak of the remarkable prosperity of the Sistan which is now known principally for its deserts covered with moving sand dunes rising to a height of 20 meters. Some experts have concluded these may be the fastest moving sand dunes anywhere in the world.

The United Nations has defined eight regions for their assistance planning: Northeast--Badakhshan, Takhar, Kunduz, Baghlan; North--Samangan, Balkh, Saripul, Jawzjan; West-- Faryab, Badghis, Herat, Farah; East-Central--Bamiyan, Ghor; Central--Kapisa, Parwan, Kabul, Logar, Wardak; East--Kunar, Nuristan, Laghman, Nangarhar; South--Paktya, Pakteka, Khost, Ghazni; Southwest--Zabul, Uruzgan, Kandahar, Hilmand, Nimroz. This reflects the creation since 1978 of three new provinces-- Saripul, Khost and Nuristan--bringing the 1996 total to thirty-two.

Construction of a circular road system to link these regions was assiduously promoted during the 1960s: with assistance from the United States south of the Hindukush, the Soviet Union north of the Hindukush, and West Germany in Paktya Province. These roads connected major cities with the principal border crossings: from Herat to Iran and Turkmenistan in the west; from Kandahar to Pakistan in the south; from Kabul through Jalalabad to Pakistan in the east; from Balkh to Uzbekistan in the north.

Other roads are unpaved, and the once-paved roads have been almost totally destroyed. This is a major impediment to reconstruction since any improvements, particularly in the agriculture sector, are hampered by the lack of an efficient deliveryinfrastructure. Rebuilding of the roads, however, is beyond the capacity of any agency now involved in Afghanistan's rehabilitation. This is the one sector that will require massive inputs which can only be obtained by such organizations as the World Bank or the Asian Bank, both of which insist on peace before becoming involved.

The plate-tectonic activity in Afghanistan has contributed to the creation of the geologic riches of the country, but has also produced frequent earthquakes; around fifty are recorded each year. Although most are relatively mild, the most severe earthquake in recent history occurred on 29 July 1985. French scientists recorded a measurement of 7.3 on the Richter scale at its epicenter in the Hindukush. Since then, according to the United States Geological Survey, there have been ten earthquakes in Afghanistan which have registered above 6.0; the most severe, both registering at 6.4, occurred in January and July 1991.

Climate

The climate is typical of an arid or semiarid steppe, with cold winters and dry summers. The mountain regions of the northeast are subarctic with dry and cold winters. In the mountains bordering Pakistan, a divergent fringe effect of the monsoon, generally coming from the southeast, brings tropical air masses that determine the climate between July and September. At times, these air masses advance into central and southern Afghanistan, bringing increased humidity and some rain.

On the intermountain plateaus the winds do not blow very strongly, but in the Sistan Basin there are severe blizzards that occur during the winter, generally December through February. In the western and southern regions a northerly wind, known as the

94

"wind of 120 days," blows during the summer months of June to September. This wind is usually accompanied by intense heat, drought, and sand storms, bringing much hardship to the inhabitants of the desert and steppe lands. Dust and whirlwinds frequently occur during the summer months on the flats in the southern part of the country. Rising at midday or in the early afternoon, these "dust winds" advance at velocities ranging between 97 and 177 kilometers per hour, raising high clouds of dust.

Temperature and precipitation are controlled by the exchange of air masses. The highest temperatures and the lowest precipitation prevail in the drought-ridden, poorly watered southern plateau region, which extends over the boundaries with Iran and Pakistan.

The Central Mountains, with higher peaks ascending toward the Pamir Knot, represent another distinct climatic region. From the Koh-e Baba Range to the Pamir Knot, January temperatures may drop to -15 C or lower in the highest mountain areas; July temperatures vary between 0 and 26 C depending on altitude. In the mountains the annual mean precipitation, much of which is snowfall, increases eastward and is highest in the Koh-e Baba Range, the western part of the Pamir Knot, and the Eastern Hindukush. Precipitation in these regions and the eastern monsoon area is about forty centimeters per year. The eastern monsoon area encompasses patches in the eastern border area with Pakistan, in irregular areas in eastern Afghanistan from north of Asmar to just north of Darkh-e Yahya, and occasionally as far west as the Kabul Valley. The Wakhan Corridor, however, which has temperatures ranging from 9 C in the summer to below -21 C in the winter, receives fewer than ten centimeters of rainfall annually. Permanent snow covers the highest mountain peaks. In the mountainous region adjacent to northern Pakistan, the snow is often more than two meters deep during the winter months. Valleys often become snow traps as the high winds sweep much of the snow from mountain peaks and ridges.

Precipitation generally fluctuates greatly during the course of the year in all parts of the country. Surprise rainstorms often transform the episodically flowing rivers and streams from puddles to torrents; unwary invading armies have been trapped in such flooding more than once in Afghanistan's history. Nomadic and seminomadic Afghans have also succumbed to the sudden flooding of their camps.

The climate of the Turkistan Plains, which extend northward from the Northern Foothills, represents a transition between mountain and steppe climates. Aridity increases and temperatures rise with descending altitudes, becoming the highest along the lower Amu Darya and in the western parts of the plains.

[RESERVED]

POPULATION

No comprehensive census based upon systematically sound methods has ever been taken in Afghanistan. Most population statistics rely on estimates and samples. Successive governments have manipulated figures for their own political objectives. UN agencies, hundreds of NGOs, as well as bilateral agencies use different figures to suit their purposes in designing assistance programs. Furthermore, instability caused by the Soviet-Afghan war and the subsequent civil war resulted in massive movements of uprooted peoples. These factors also make demographic sampling necessarily imprecise.

The most scientific demographic survey carried out in Afghanistan was also one of the first. Conducted in 1972-74 by the State University of New York (SUNY) for the United States Agency for International Development (AID), in cooperation with the Afghan government, this survey reported a settled population of 10.18 million. It did not cover the entire country, and the nomadic population was not surveyed. The nomads were separately estimated at slightly more than 1 million.

An official census was later hurriedly taken over a three-week period in June 1979 after the establishment of the People's Democratic Party of Afghanistan (PDPA), with UN assistance. This count estimated the population to be 13.9 million, including 800,000 nomads, but it is little credited since only 56 percent of the population was enumerated due to mounting resistance in the countryside. Grossly inflated figures were added for the rest.

The *Statistical Yearbook* published in 1983 by the Babrak Karmal government during the Soviet occupation claimed a total population of 15.96 million for 1981-82. Presumably this included over five million refugees in Pakistan and Iran. (see Refugees, this ch.).

Afghanistan's population in 1995 was estimated at 18.4 million by the Population Reference Bureau, a nonprofit agency based in Washington, D.C. This estimate, like others before it, is based on unreliable data, as the Bureau itself cautions. The *Human Development Report, 1996* estimates that the population will rise to 26.7 million in the year 2000, using, however, a high growth rate of 6.1 percent. A rate of around 2.2 percent is more typically employed. UNDP calculations give a 1993 crude birth rate of 51/1000, a crude death rate of 22/1000, and an infant mortality rate of 163/1000. Estimates of the average life expectancy at birth was 43.7 years. Again, growth figures depend on what is taken into account -- refugees, war dead estimated to range from three-quarters of a million to a million and a half, birth and death rates -- all of which are open to question.

The average population density was calculated in 1993 at 23.4 per square kilometer, but it varied widely between provinces: from 489.4 per square kilometer in Kabul to 0.7 in Nimroz, a province in the southwest with vast sandy and stony deserts. Residence was also unevenly distributed between rural and urban settlements, with over 35,000 rural settlements, but only sixty-four urban centers. Probably no more than ten of these centers are true cities, and other towns could be considered. Again, numbers depend on definitions. The United Nations reported that eighty-one percent of the population lived in rural areas in 1993.

What is important is that the gradual rural-urban migration noticeable over a period of several decades increased rapidly during the 1960s as the government laid out new road systems and quickened development. This trend accelerated during the Soviet-Afghan War as internally displaced persons (IDPs) fled the war-torn countryside for the relative safety of the cities. A number of major cities such as Kabul, Ghazni, Jalalabad, and Mazar-e Sharif absorbed IDPs in great numbers, causing overcrowding and rising demands for city-provided services. By 1985, unconfirmed reports placed Kabul's population at over two million, more than a 100 percent increase in less than a decade. Since the mujahidin took possession of Kabul in 1992, however, the incessant fighting by warring factions for control of the capital has caused the population to swell and diminish according to the level of security at any given moment.

SOCIAL STRUCTURE

Afghanistan is home to a multiplicity of ethnic and linguistic groups, as well as several sects within Islam and other religions. Historic and geographic factors created and preserved this diversity although varying degrees of cultural assimilation continuously take place and a considerable degree of cultural homogeneity exists.

Ethnicity has been extensively explored by scholars; they often disagree. Any simple classification is bound to have exceptions for Afghan society has never been static within fixed boundaries. The picture has been drawn and redrawn throughout the course of its history.

Further, ethnicity means different things to different groups. Every group uses the identification term *qaum* to explain a complexity of affiliations, a network, of families or occupations. Each has a rich density of meanings. Every individual belongs to a *qaum* which provides protection from outside encroachments, cooperation, support, security, and assistance, either social, political or economic. Frequently a village corresponds to a *qawm*, but it does not necessarily exist in a precise geographic setting. In a more restricted sense *qaum* refers to descent groups, from family kin to ethnic group. In tribal areas *qaum* refers to a common genealogy from extended family, or clan, to tribe to tribal confederation. Most simply, *qawm* defines an individual's identity in his social world.

Ethnic Groups

In 1996, approximately 40 percent of Afghans were Pashtun, 11.4 of whom are of the Durrani tribal group and 13.8 percent of the Ghilzai group. Tajiks make up the second largest ethnic group with 25.3 percent of the population, followed by Hazaras, 18 percent; Uzbeks, 6.3 percent; Turkmen, 2.5 percent; Qizilbash, 1.0; 6.9 percent other. The usual caveat regarding statistics is particularly appropriate here.

Pashtun

The largest and traditionally most politically powerful ethnic group, the Pashtun (or Pakhtun in northern Pakhtu dialects), is composed of many units totalling in 1995 an estimated 10.1 million, the most numerous being the Durrani and the Ghilzai. Other major tribes include the Wardak, Jaji, Tani, Jadran, Mangal, Khugiani, Safi, Mohmand and Shinwari. Like a number of other Afghan ethnic groups, the Pushtun extend beyond Afghanistan into Pakistan where they constitute a major ethnic group of about 14 million.

The Afghan Pushtun heartland roughly covers a large crescent-shaped belt following the Afghan-Pakistani border on the east, southward from Nuristan, across the south, and northward along the Iranian border almost to Herat. Enclaves of Pashtun also live scattered among other ethnic groups throughout the nation, where they have settled at various times since the end of the nineteenth century as shifts in populations, some forced, some voluntary, occurred in response to political expediency and economic opportunities (see Abdur Rahman Khan, 1880-1901, ch.1).

Physically the Pushtun are basically a Mediterranean variant of the greater Caucasian race and speak several mutually intelligible dialects of Pashtu; some also speak Dari. Both Pashtu and Dari belong to the Iranian branch of the Indo-European language family. Pushtun are generally Hanafi Sunni Muslims, but some are Ithna Asharia Shia (see Ithna Asharia, this ch.).

The Pushtun have provided the central leadership for Afghanistan since the eighteenth century when Ahmad Khan Abdali of Kandahar established the Durrani Empire. This one-time general in Nadir Shah's Persian army was elected to power in 1747 at a tribal *jirgah*, an assembly which takes decisions by consensus. The legitimacy of his rule was sanctioned at the same time by the *ulama* (religious scholars) (see Ahmad Shah and the Durrani Empire, ch.1). Ahmad Khan assumed the title of *Durr-i-Durran* (Pearl of Pearls) and was henceforth known as Ahmad Shah Durrani and his tribe, the Pushtun Abdali tribe, as the Durrani. When his successors lost the support of the tribes after Ahmad Shah's death in 1772, control passed to the Mohammadzai lineage within the Barakzai section of the Durrani Pushtun.

Mohammadzai dominance continued from 1826 to 1978, interrupted only for a scant nine months in 1929. Then power shifted to the second largest Pushtun tribe, the Ghilzai, who dominated the leadership of the secular Democratic Republic of Afghanistan (DRA) after 1978, although most were essentially detribalized because of their close association with urban life. This regime was in turn replaced in 1992 by the Islamic State of Afghanistan, established by the mujahidin whose leaders were mostly from the Ghilzai, and a variety of eastern Pushtun tribes, although the President from 1992-1996 was a Tajik. This state has been challenged since the October 1994 takeover of Kandahar by the Pushtun Taliban. The Taliban heartland remains in the south and while the original leadership bid for unity by playing down tribal identities, divisions began to surface after Kabul was taken in September 1996.

Pushtun culture rests on *Pushtunwali*, a legal and moral code that determines social order and responsibilities. It contains sets of values pertaining to honor (*namuz*), solidarity (*nang*), hospitality, mutual support, shame and revenge which determines social order and individual responsibility. The defence of *namuz*, even unto death, is obligatory for every Pushtun. Elements in this code of behavior are often in opposition to the Shariah. Much of the resistance to the largely detribalized leadership of the DRA stemmed from the perception that in attempting to nationalize land and wealth, as well as regulate marriage practices, the DRA was unlawfully violating the prescriptions of *Pushtunwali*.

The Pushtun are basically farmers or herdsmen, or combinations of both, although several groups are renowned for specialized occupations. For instance, the monarchy and many government bureaucrats were Durrani Pushtun, the Ahmadzai Ghilzai are consulted for their legal abilities, the Andar Ghilzai specialize in constructing and repairing underground irrigation systems called *karez*, and the Shinwari of Paktya monopolize the lumber trade. Pushtun nomads are discussed below.

Tajik

The Tajik form the second largest ethnic group in Afghanistan. Estimates in 1995 averaged around 4.3 million. Afghan Tajik live mainly in the Panjsher Valley north of Kabul and in the northern and northeastern provinces of Parwan, Takhar, Badakhshan, and also Baghlan and Samangan. Tajik also extend into the central mountains. There is a tendency of some non-Tajik groups to classify any Dari speaker as a member of this group. Some also tend to categorize any urban resident who has become detribalized as Tajik. This is particularly true in Kabul. Tajik are also found north of Afghanistan's border in their own state of Tajikistan.

Tajik are physically from the Mediterranean substock. They speak various Tajiki dialects of Dari, an Iranian language in the Indo-European language family. Most are Hanafi Sunni, although a sizeable number living in areas from Bamiyan to eastern Badakhshan are Ismaili Shia. Tajik are not organized by tribe and

106

refer to themselves most often by the name of the valley or region they inhabit, such as Panjsheri, Andarabi, Samangani, and Badakhshi. Those living among non-Tajik, such as those living among the Pushtun who refer to them as *dehqan*, often describe themselves simply as Tajik.

Tajik are predominantly fully sedentary mountaineer farmers and herders, who often make short-range seasonal migrations to alpine grazing meadows during which whole families move up to the mountains to harvest grain and melons. The Tajik areas are famous for a wide variety of fruits and nuts which are acknowledged to be among the finest in the country.

Many Tajik migrated to the cities, especially to Kabul, which was primarily a Tajik town until Timur, the son of Ahmad Shah Durrani, moved his court to Kabul in 1776 and declared it to be the Pushtun capital. In Kabul the Tajik are still dominant and well-represented in the uppermiddle class. Many are active in business and in government service; others find employment as cooks, houseboys or gardeners in the homes of foreigners. On the off-agricultural season Tajik may join the workforce at industrial complexes near their villages. Whether seasonally or permanently based in cities, Tajik tend to maintain close links with their rural kin.

Except for the short rule of the Tajik known as Bacha Saqqao in 1928, the Tajik have not dominated politically. Since 1978, however, several Tajik military leaders have gained substantial recognition, the most renowned being Ahmad Shah Masood from the Panjsher Valley. Burhanuddin Rabbani who served as President of The Islamic State of Afghanistan from 1992-1996 is a Tajik from Badakhshan.

Hazara

Afghanistan's rugged central mountainous core of approximately 50,000 square kilometers is known as the Hazarajat, Land of the Hazara. Others live in Badakhshan, and, following Kabul's campaigns against them in the late nineteenth century, some settled in western Turkestan, in Jauzjan and Badghis provinces. Estimated population in 1995 was one million.

Physically the Hazara are Mongoloid, possibly of mixed Eastern Turkic and Mongol origin, although numerous contradictory speculations exist. Scholars agree that the Hazara were established here since the beginning of the thirteenth century. Hazara speak Hazaragi, a Persianized language with a large mixture of Mongol words. A majority are Imami Shia; fewer are Ismaili Shia; while others, particularly in Bamiyan and the north, are Sunni.

The leaders of Hazara lineages, known as *mirs* or *khans*, lost their powerful status in communities after Amir Abdur Rahman subdued them in 1891. The Pushtun state established a local administration, imposed harsh taxation policies and distributed lands to Pushtun, including fertile pasture lands in areas previously inaccessible to Pushtun nomads.

The Hazarajat continued to be a neglected area. Services and physical infrastructure were practically nonexistent. Farming and animal husbandry are the principal occupations; there is no industry. Because of their meager resources, the Hazara seasonally sought work and services in other areas as low grade civil servants, shopkeepers, artisans, urban factory workers, and unskilled labour. In the 1960s an estimated 30-50 percent of Hazara males migrated to the cities where they were considered to be on the lowest rung of the social scale. During the 1960s and 70s their economic and political status improved remarkably.

During the war, contending groups within the Hazarajat achieved greater unity than ever before. Hazara political parties were excluded from the *mujahideen* alliances, however, largely because of rabidly anti-Shia prejudices held by some leaders, such as Abdur Rab Rasul Sayyaf and Yunus Khalis. It is doubtful if the Hazara will accept their former inferior status in the future.

Uzbek

About 1.3 million Uzbek live mingled with the Tajik all across the northern plains of Afghanistan, from Faryab Province to Faizabad, capital of Badakhshan Province. There are many mixed Uzbek and Tajik villages, although each live in separate residential quarters. In 1983 a sizeable group of Uzbek were included among the group of 4,000 Turkic speakers from Afghanistan that were resettled in Turkey. Uzbek also reside north of the Afghan border in Uzbekistan, Tajikistan and Turkmenistan.

The Uzbek are Mongoloid with considerable Mediterranean admixture. They are Sunni Muslim and speak central Turkic dialects called Uzbeki. Uzbek practice agriculture and herding, but many live in towns where they are known as astute businessmen and skillful artisans as silver and goldsmiths, leatherworkers, and rug makers.

Some Afghan Uzbek refer to themselves by old tribal names; others identify with their towns of origin in Central Asia. Uzbek social structure is strictly patriarchal, giving considerable authoritarian power to leaders called *begs*, *arbabs* or *khans*. Marital endogamy is of prime importance. Although interethnic marriages between Uzbek, Turkoman and Tajik do take place, antipathy to marriage with Pushtun is widespread.

Afghan Uzbek originally came from Central Asia and their rise as the dominant political force in north Afghanistan followed the demise in 1506 of the Timurid dynasty centered at Herat. They established eleven strong principalities from Maimana to Kunduz under strong leaders, sometimes independent, sometimes nominally acknowledging allegiance to either Bokhara or Kabul, but always jockeying for power among themselves.

At the end of the nineteenth century Amir Abdur Rahman consolidated these Uzbak khanates under his rule. Later, fresh immigrations took place in the 1920s and 1930s as Russian conquests and local uprisings in Central Asia continued. During this same period many Pushtun settled among the Uzbeks with the result that by the 1960s the Uzbek had become a small minority within the area they once dominated. Since 1992, the Uzbek General Abdul Rashid Dostom, principal leader of the coalition opposing the Taliban, has controlled the predominant centers of power in the north.

Turkmen

Turkmen are another Sunni Turkic-speaking group whose language has close affinities with modern Turkish. They are of aquiline Mongoloid stock. The Afghan Turkmen population in the 1990s is estimated at around 200,000. Turkmen also reside north of the Amu Darya in Turkmenistan. The original Turkmen groups came from east of the Caspian Sea into northwestern Afghanistan at various periods, particularly after the end of the nineteenth century when the Russians moved into their territory. They established settlements from Balkh Province to Herat Province, where they are now concentrated; smaller groups settled in Kunduz Province. Others came in considerable numbers as a result of the failure of the Basmachi revolts against the Bolsheviks in the 1920s.

Turkmen tribes, of which there are twelve major groups in Afghanistan, base their structure on genealogies traced through the male line. Senior members wield considerable authority. Formerly a nomadic and warlike people feared for their lightening raids on caravans, Turkmen in Afghanistan are farmer-herdsmen and important contributors to the economy. They brought karakul sheep to Afghanistan and are also renowned makers of carpets, which, with karakul pelts, are major hard currency export commodities. Turkmen jewelry is also highly prized.

Other Groups

Aimaq

Aimaq, meaning tribe in Turkish, is not an ethnic domination, but differentiates seminomadic herders and agricultural tribal groups of various ethnic origins, including the Turkic Hazara and Baluch, that were formed in the sixteenth and seventeenth centuries. They live among nontribal people in the western areas of Badghis, Ghor and Herat provinces. They are Sunni, speak dialects close to Dari and refer to themselves with tribal designations. Population estimates vary widely, from less than 500,000 to around 800,000. A group of about 120,000 live in Iranian Khorasan.

Arab

Large groups of Sunni Arab living in the vicinity of Bokhara in Central Asia fled to northeastern Afghanistan following Russian conquests in the nineteenth century. By the 1880s they were, with the Uzbek with whom they established close ties, the second most populous ethnic group in present day Kunduz, Takhar and Baghlan provinces. Smaller groups settled in scattered communities as far west as Maimana, Faryab Province.

The Arab are pastoralists who raise sheep and grow cotton and wheat. Some among the eastern groups make summer migrations of up to 300 kilometers to reach the lush high pastures in Badakhshan. Government development schemes, especially those which brought large numbers of Pushtun to the area in the 1940s, relegated the Arab to a small proportion of the population and the Arab ceased to hold a monopoly on long distance migration. Bilingual in Dari and Uzbeki, but speaking no Arabic, they continue to identify themselves as Arab although they have had no contact with the Arabs of the Middle East since the late fourteenth century.

Kirghiz

The Kirghiz are a Sunni Mongoloid group speaking Kipchak Turkic dialects who were originally from Central Asia. About 3,000 lived in the Pamir mountains east of the Wakhan Corridor, one of the more inaccessible regions in the world where relatively flat valleys suitable for habitation lie at altitudes over 10,000 feet between ranges rising over 16,500 feet. Only a small group remains. A majority moved to Pakistan in 1978 after Soviet and Afghan troops occupied the Wakhan; later, in 1983, resettled in Turkey.

The Kirghiz lived in yurts, tended large flocks of sheep and utilized yak which are found only in this area of Afghanistan.

Wakhi

The neighboring Wakhi, along with several thousand other Mountain Tajik who are physically of the Mediterranean substock with Mongoloid admixture, speak Dari and various eastern Iranian dialects. They live in small, remote villages located at lower altitudes in the Wakhan Corridor and upper Badakhshan. They are often Ismaili Shi'a, but some are Imami Shi'a and Sunni.

Farsiwan

Farsiwan are Dari-speaking village agriculturalists of Mediterranean substock who live in the west near the Afghan-Iranian border or in districts of Herat, Kandahar and Ghazni provinces. Estimates for 1995 vary from 600,000 to 830,000. Most are Imami Shi'a; in urban centers some are Sunni.

Nuristani

The Nuristani reside throughout a 5,000 square mile area in the east bordering Pakistan that is heavily forested and so rugged that much of it is accessible only by foot trails. The Nuristani designate themselves by the local geographical names of the five major north-south valleys and 30 east-west lateral valleys leading into the major valleys where they live. They speak Indo-Iranian dialects of Nuristani and Dardic called by village and valley names; many are mutually unintelligible from valley to valley. In 1990 the province of Nuristan was created from parts of the provinces of Laghman and Kunar. The population in the 1990s is estimated at 125,000 by some; the Nuristani prefer a figure of 300,000.

The Nuristani are of the Mediterranean physical type with mixtures from Indian stocks on the fringes. Historians accompanying Alexander the Great in the fourth century BC described this group as differing culturally and religiously from other peoples in the area. They were forcibly converted to Sunni Islam in 1895 during the reign of Amir Abdur Rahman but retain many unique features in their material culture.

The Nuristani are mountaineer herders, dairymen and farmers. They hold a respected place in the social order and many have risen to high government positions, particularly in the army.

Baluch

The homeland of the Sunni Baluch in southwestern Afghanistan is in the sparsely settled deserts and semi-deserts of Hilmand Province, although Baluch enclaves are also found in northwestern Faryab Province. These semisedentary and seminomadic populations are famed for camel breeding. They number perhaps around 100,000, although other estimates are lower. Seventy percent of the Baluch live in Pakistan; others reside in Iran. The Baluch speak Baluchi, an Iranian branch in the Indo-European language family; most speak Dari and Pashto as well. Baluch society is tribal, highly segmented and centrally organized under powerful chieftains known as *sardars*.

Brahui

The Sunni Brahui is another distinctive group settled in the desert areas of southwestern Afghanistan. They numbered about 200,000 in 1970 according to an estimate by Louis Dupree; estimates in the 1990s run lower. The basic Brahui physical type is Veddoid of South India, and they speak Brahui which is allied to Dravidian, a major language of South India, with a heavy mixture of Balulchi and Pashto. Brahui mostly work as tenant farmers or hired herders for Baluch or Pushtun khans. Larger communities of Brahui reside in Pakistan's Baluchistan Province.

Qizilbash

The Qizilbash of Mediterranean sub-stock speak Dari, are Imami Shi'a, and scattered throughout Afghanistan, primarily in urban centers. There are perhaps 50,000 Qizilbash living in Afghanistan although it is difficult to say for some claim to be Sunni Tajik since Shia Islam permits the practice of *taqiya* or dissimulation to avoid religious discrimination. The Qizilbash form one of the more literate groups in Afghanistan; they hold important administrative and professional positions.

The Qizilbash are traditionally considered to be the descendants of Persian Shia mercenaries and administrators left behind by the Safavid Emperor Nadir Shah Afshar (1736-47) to govern the Afghan provinces. Under Ahmad Shah Durrani, who served in Nadir Shah's bodyguard, and his successors, the Qizilbash acquired power and influence at court out of proportion to their numbers. This created resentment among the dominant Pushtun which hardened over the years, especially after the Qizilbash openly allied themselves with the British during the First Anglo-Afghan War (1838-1842). Amir Abdur Rahman accused the Qizilbash of being partisan to the enemy during his campaigns against the Shi'a Hazara in 1891-1893, declared them enemies of the state, confiscated their property and persecuted them.

Kabuli

Kabuli, is an ambiguous term which provides a sense of identity for Afghanistan's largest heterogeneous urban population without designating distinct ethnic associations. The city of Kabul has drawn members of all ethnic groups in growing numbers since 1776 when it was declared the capital in favor of Kandahar; generations of intermarriages have also taken place. Nevertheless, ethnic roots and regional links have always also remained important. This is reflected in the spatial layout of the city which, before two-thirds of the city was reduced to rubble after 1992, consisted of ethnic, geographic or religious-oriented wards and suburbs. Social stratification along occupational lines was also clear although over the past few decades lines tended to blur significantly.

A typical Kabuli speaks Dari in addition to his mother tongue and, whether male or female, is urbane, favors European fashions, is secularly educated, and most probably works as a bureaucrat, shopkeeper/owner or in the service sector. Many have had professional education or experience abroad, live in apartments or single-family dwellings, are Western-oriented in outlook and enjoy cosmopolitan lifestyles. It is this image which conservatives, especially those such as the rural Taliban find unpalatable, a symbol of moral degradation which must be eradicated if a truly Islamic state is to be established in Afghanistan.

Many Kabuli who remained in Kabul during the Soviet-Afghan War have since left because they find the attitudes of the new leadership incompatible. They are now displaced in cities inside Afghanistan, living as refugees in Pakistan or resettled abroad. Their absence will severely hinder the reestablishment of viable administrative and economic systems necessary for the reconstruction and development of Afghanistan.

116

Jat

There are other small marginal communities of occupational specialists based in eastern Afghanistan in provinces such as Laghman. They are commonly referred to as Jat which is a generic term indiscriminately applied by others with derogatory connotations implying low descent and low occupations. The groups reject the term and refer to themselves by specific names. Of Mediterranean-Indian type physically, speaking Indo-Aryan dialects in addition to Pashto and Dari, they are primarily gypsy-like itinerant petty traders, bangle sellers, fortune-tellers, musicians, jugglers, snake-charmers and performers with animals such as bears and monkeys. Some are specialized craftsmen, working as weavers, potters, sievemakers, knife-makers, and leather-workers. Some hire out as seasonal itinerant farm laborers. They rank lowest on the social scale and are stigmatized by many in the society.

Non-Muslims

Hindus and Sikhs live mostly in urban centers throughout Afghanistan. They are merchants and moneylenders. In 1978 they numbered about 30,000. Many left in 1992, but are slowly returning to such cities as Ghazni and Jalalabad. The Jewish community of Kabul is totally depleted. One family remains in 1996 to care for the synagogue which partially remains in an area otherwise pulverized.

Interethnic Relations

Afghanistan's ethnic mosaic has no precise boundaries; nor is its national culture uniform. Few of its ethnic groups are indigenous; few maintain racial homogeneity. Many zones overlap and interactions broadened as the economic infrastructure improved and educational opportunities widened.

Resentment rising out of wars and conquests remains long after the power of conquerors dissipates. This is true with regard to the Uzbeks. The distrust and discrimination between Hazara and Pushtun set during late nineteenth century confrontations is still abundantly present. The causes of prejudice against the Qizilbash go back to the eighteenth century.

Kabul's political policies also had long-term effects in aggravating ethnic tensions. This is most evident in the successive movements of thousands of Pushtun into the northern areas, beginning with the forced relocations of Amir Abdur Rahman's Pushtun opponents in the late nineteenth century and again employed as late as 1947-1949 following revolts among the Safi Pushtun in eastern Afghanistan. Competition with local populations occasioned considerable stress.

Equally significant were the effects of successful land reclamation projects, beginning in the 1930s, which offered attractive incentives to new settlers. These invariably favored the Pushtun over local populations. The land settlement schemes in the Hilmand in the southwest, begun in 1910 and massively extended after 1946, were similarly disruptive. Settlers from all parts of Afghanistan were recruited into this predominantly Pushtun and Baluch area, creating new tensions not only among the new disparate groups, but also among new and old Pushtun groups.

Local conflicts in all areas, within all groups, most often erupt over disputes concerning property or access to resources, whether it be land, water, money, business or government opportunities, bridewealth or inheritance. Naturally evolving demographic pressures accompanied by competition form the basis of other conflicts. Also, the tendency of past governments to initiate policies enhancing Pushtun prominence, increased the traditional Pushtun military and numerical dominance which allowed them to assert their will over other ethnic groups and maintain their status as the nation's most prestigious group.

Thus, there have always been tensions between groups, from petty squabbles to feuds lasting for generations, rising from a variety of causes but rarely from intrinsic attitudes of ethnic discrimination. Considering the disparate and volatile ingredients that exist, Afghanistan's history records remarkably few internal explosions that are specifically focussed on ethnicity.

During the Soviet-Afghan War, the shared goals of the *mujahidin*--opposition to nonbelieving atheist invaders and group solidarity--were reminiscent of familial, tribal, and ethnic group construction. As such, the appeal of the *mujahidin* was a strong and familiar rallying cry and source of solidarity for Afghans in their struggle for national liberation.

Afghan ethnic identities emerged more clearly during the Soviet-Afghan War. Five groups could be easily distinguished: Tajik, including all Sunni Dari speakers; Hazara; Uzbek; Durrani Pushtun; Ghilzai Pushtun and Eastern Pushtun. Fighting among Afghans in the years following the fall of Najibullah's government in 1992 exceeded levels of violence experienced even during the wars of Amir Abdur Rahman against the Hazara and the Nuristani between 1891 and 1896. Some would say that these conflicts are evidence that Afghan society must now be fragmented between groups identified by religious, ethnic, or regional labels. There is no doubt that the Soviet-Afghan War severely disturbed the delicate social infrastructure constructed over many centuries, yet according to many Afghans the present turmoil is driven more by political greed and external interference than by ethnic, religious or regional considerations. While traditional structures were not equitable for all Afghan citizens, they did permit extended periods of civic stability. Even in the mid-1990s, there was ample evidence in a number of areas outside the present arenas of conflict to suggest that a return to the old order could occur.

Elements of material culture are used by all ethnic groups to build pride and a sense of social superiority, particularly in mixed ethnic zones. The Nuristani are the most unique in dress, diet and architecture. In other areas distinctions have softened over the years as the improved infrastructure encouraged greater mobility.

The most striking differences are noted in dress, particularly in headgear. Turbans are characteristic of the Pashtun. The shape of caps, round, conical or peaked, their material and decoration are distinctive indicators between and within many groups. *Chapan*, loose sometimes quilted coats of cotton or silk with stripes of varied colors to indicate specific regions, are worn in the north; *pattu*, shawls, are preferred in the south. For women, color, the width of the skirt, and the type of embroidery are meaningful distinctions.

Diet also changes from group to group, although bread and tea are dietary staples everywhere. Some bread is round, some oval; some prefer black tea, others green. The Uzbek include many pasta dishes in their cuisine. Dwellings of sedentary groups, mostly made from pressed mud or sun-dried brick, may be domed or flat-roofed, modestly enclosed behind walls or hidden within towering fortress-like enclosures, although open villages do exist in the Hazarajat. Tents used by the nomads vary in shape, material and structure from group to group.

Each group uses folktales to reinforce the uniqueness and superiority of the one over the other, as well as to describe their individual ideals.

Tribes

Tribalism is not a feature of every ethnic group in Afghanistan; and even within tribally organized groups tribalism is a flexible concept that allows variations to exist and changes to occur as kinship groups rise and fall.

Tribal identity which merges with ethnicity rests on unified genealogies consisting of descendants of a common male ancestor whose name often provides the name of the group. Internal divisions consist of the descendants of intermediate descendants of the original founder. Thus an entire tribe may descend from a man ten or more generations in the past. Smaller segmentary patrilineages composed of great-grandsons and grandsons form units of residence and strong personal loyalty.

Although preferred marriages for males are to father's brother's daughters, genealogies reflect political, economic and social alliances outside strict descent lines. Typically, it is men from dominant groups who will seek to marry with females outside their own ethnic group.

The Pushtun represent the largest tribal entities in Afghanistan; among them tribal institutions are strongest within the Ghilzai. Common characteristics of Pushtun tribal organization ideally feature egalitarianism, democratic decision-making through councils called *jirgah* at which individual members have the right to express themselves freely, and certain corporate responsibilities such as revenge. Revenge, for instance, may be taken on any member of an offending tribe, although liability is usually greater for those most closely related to the accused. The essentially decentralized independent communities within tribal subsections conduct both internal and external affairs according to the tribal code of conduct called Pushtunwali (see Pushtun, this ch.).

The aristocratic elites who lead subdivisions, rise to their positions primarily through personal charisma, patronage, and leadership abilities rather than by primogeniture, which is not recognized in Muslim law, or any type of prescribed hereditary rights. Tribal organization is therefore acephalous or without a paramount chief. And the measure of their power differs. Heads of nomadic tribal groups, for instance, act principally as spokesmen, but have no right to make decisions binding on others.

The absence of recognized principles governing the assumption of leadership allows for intense competition. Rivalries within and between tribal segments and between tribes and subtribes consequently have always existed. It is these internecine feuds that have earned the Pushtun their reputation as an unruly and warlike people. Nonetheless, when outside forces threaten, the Pushtun are equally reputed for their ability to forge formidable alliances, among themselves and with other ethnic groups.

Both internal as well as intergroup conflicts are most often rooted in matters of personal and group honour, personal enmities, family dissensions concerning brides and property, struggles for material possession, access to resources, territorial integrity and extensions of power, rather than in intrinsic attitudes of ethnic discrimination.

Many contentious struggles raged about the creation of the nation-state. Although Ahmad Shah Durrani set the stage for Pushtun dominance, his successors lacked both his personal charisma and his leadership abilities. His son, Timur Shah (1772-1783), further compounded the problem by leaving behind 23 sons born of wives from ten different tribes without designating a successor. Similarly, the next charismatic leader to consolidate the area, Amir Dost Mohammad (1834-38; 1842-63), left 20 sons to fight for the throne. Violent episodes involving individual quests for power characterized much of the eighteenth and nineteenth centuries.

With the advent of Amir Abdur Rahman (1880-1901), a grandson of Amir Doṣt Mohammad, the situation changed dramatically. Amir Abdur Rahman utilized his powerful personality in combination with adroit politics and judicious use of financial subsidies and weaponry provided by the British. To further his ambition to establish a centralized state under his authoritarian control, he created the first standing army and relied heavily on the support of his own Mohammadzai section of the Barakzai Durrani, to whom he granted annual allowances. Thus he raised the Mohammadzai to a privileged group and reduced the power of the tribal Sardars. At his death in 1901 he was succeeded by his son without the usual violent upheavals.

State institution building was met with periodic open revolts such as that of the eastern Pushtun which ended the rule of King Amanullah in 1929. King Nadir (1929-1933) restored the preeminence of central Mohammadzai control with tribal assistance. The 1978 coup d'etat deposed the Mohammadzai and the Soviet-Afghan War introduced political parties which brought new leadership patterns into being, altering tribal structures and reshaping ethnic identities. Traditional segmentation has not disappeared, but it is now being expressed through new political structures.

MODES OF SUBSISTENCE

Afghans have developed a number of different strategies to wrest a living from their difficult, often marginal environment. Some pastoralist or herdsmen groups live a seasonally nomadic existence although other herding communities are sedentary. Often groups combine animal husbandry with agriculture; some rely very little on livestock. These subsistence patterns are to some extent fluid, pastoralists often changing their degree of reliance on cultivation, depending on ecological, economic, and political factors.

Pastoralism

Afghanistan has fine pastures permitting a considerable portion of its population, perhaps 9 percent, to engage in nomadic pastoralism. This entails annual migrations with large flocks of sheep and goats from lowland winter settlements, where they sow and reap crops and live in housing of a fairly permanent nature, to highland summer pastures located above 1,000 meters; sometimes as high as 3,500 meters. Here they occupy fixed grazing grounds which they do not own but on which they have traditional grazing rights. Sometimes they pay a fee. Other nomadic groups practice various types of trading. Uniquely adapted to the environment, pastoral nomads help maintain the nation's ecosystem and contribute substantially to the national economy.

Estimates of nomadic populations are even more uncertain than those for settled populations. The figure of 1.5 million given in many official publications in 1996 is an average of 1970 estimates which varied from 800,00 to over 2.5 million. Again the wide range results from differences in definition and from the fact that changes brought about by displacement and war have yet to be adequately analyzed. Fully nomadic groups were always rare. Some groups are semi-nomadic. In their case, a majority of the group moves annually from summer to winter pastures, while fewer remain behind in permanent settlements. In semi-sedentary groups, a minority participate in the migrations.

Nomadic groups are found among the Pushtun, Baluch, Aimaq, Turkmen, Arab, Uzbek, and Kirghiz; perhaps over 80 percent are Durrani and Ghilzai Pushtun, Within each of these groups, however, the nomads form a minority.

Many differences between groups have been described by leading social scientists noted in the bibliography. Yet a few patterns may be noted. During the fall and winter, nomadic groups live in permanent or temporary housing on steppes and plains; in the spring they move to lush pastures in the central mountains. The big herds that travel along high mountain trails are composed largely of sheep, including a highly valuable breed called *karakul* or Persian Lamb, a major export. Only 10-40 percent of the herds are goats because the market price for sheep is usually twice that of goats.

The flocks belong to single nuclear families from different segments of subtribes and each household will own an average of about 100 animals. Typically 4-6 households will join together to form herd units of optimum size consistent with the labor capacities of individual families and prevailing conditions of the pastures. Each herd unit is tended by a shepherd, who is paid a share of the lambs and kids born under his care.

Nuclear households grouped again by tribal segments move along lower routes more suitable for the heavily laden camels, horses and donkeys carrying household goods, women, children and the elderly. These groups, accompanied by smaller numbers of animals and guarded by fierce mastiff-like herd dogs, follow traditional routes with little variation, moving only five kilometers or so a day when travelling through grassy regions, but up to 20 kilometers a day when the terrain is barren. For some, the migration may be only a matter of a few kilometers; others move up to 500 kilometers away from their winter headquarters.

Camp sites seldom include more than 100 single household dwellings; often no more than five. These portable dwellings are of distinct shapes, including several variants of the classic rectangular black goat's hair tent predominately used by Pushtun and Baluch.

The nomads neither move nor live in isolation for they maintain relationships with both agriculturalists and merchants to whom they sell pastoral products, mainly live animals, wool, skins and dairy products, in exchange for agricultural produce, primarily cereals, household and luxury items, including radios. Poorer nomadic families may serve farmers as seasonal labor during harvest periods while richer nomads who extend credit may acquire land from farmers who, unable to pay their debts, become their tenants. Nomads also act as disseminators of local news. Large-scale trading, money lending and casual labor opportunities are often more important than herding to the eastern Ghilzai whose caravans once reached deep into India (later Pakistan) as far as what is now Bangladesh, as well as north to Bokhara, east to China, and west to Iran. These far-flung migrations which had taken place since the eleventh century virtually came to a halt after the 1930s when the Soviet Union and China sealed their borders. They experienced further curtailment after Pakistan closed its border in 1961 during the Pushtunistan dispute.

Internally, the effects of increases in population, modernization, state interventions and abnormal climatic conditions causing market prices to fall necessitated severe adjustments. For many nomads by the end of the 1970s their situation deteriorated to such an extent that they were obliged to settle down. The war exacerbated these trends. The indiscriminate dropping of mines from helicopters onto pastures is but one example. Despite this, many nomadic groups acquired significant political power because of their major roles in the resistance, particularly in the transportation of arms. They became one of the best armed groups in Afghanistan.

This laid the ground for potential tensions over settlement rights in the future as evidenced by controversies between nomadic and settled groups that arose when nomads occupied land around Khost because their traditional movement patterns had been disrupted. In resolving the issue, the Taliban were obliged to sanction the nomad occupations because of their superior strength.

Other groups have also been forced to abandon their nomadic way of life. Numbers of nomads have purchased shops in provincial centers such as Khost and Gardez. A major portion of the Kirghiz have resettled in Turkey. Among nomadic groups forming part of

refugee populations in Pakistan, few have been able to retain their flocks and the assistance community has been unable to address their special needs. Yet, among the refugees there are a few who have accumulated fabulous riches and live opulently in elite suburbs of Peshawar, Islamabad and Karachi.

Mixed Subsistence Patterns

Mixtures of pastoralism with limited migration and agriculture are very common. In all ethnic groups there are fully sedentary villages with semi-sedentary elements, such as short vertical summer migrations into the hills to graze flocks or harvest grains and melons. The picture does not remain static as the degrees of agricultural versus pastoralist strategies increases during difficult times, such as periods of drought, because of disease, or the inability to repay debts. Poorer nomads can become sedentary because they lose their flocks. On the other hand, wealthy nomads who invest in land may eventually prefer to settle in order to manage their holdings.

Sedentary populations can also take up elements of pastoralism and generate new semi-nomadic units. Farmers practicing a mixed subsistence tend to invest surpluses in enlarging their flocks which may soon overgraze lands surrounding the irrigated oases around settlements if they are not kept moving. Agriculturists with relatively large herds will therefore assign nomadic pastoralist duties to younger brothers who in time may elect to remain nomadic and relinquish land inheritance in favor of increased livestock. A new nomad family is thus born, although the process may take more than one generation.

Former nomads may also return to nomadism if, after being forced through poverty to give up herding, they manage to earn enough to start another herd. Pastoral nomadism and sedentary agriculture, therefore, are not necessarily permanent adaptations and vary in any given place at any given time.

Agricultural subsistence patterns differ with the terrain. The majority of cultivators own their own land. Holdings are typically small and there are relatively few landowners with hugh estates. But in all areas water is the most important determining factor and must be carefully managed. Because of the scarcity of water, only 10-12 percent of the surface of Afghanistan is cultivated, and of this only one-quarter is irrigated. The rest depends on vulnerable rain-fed dry farming known as *lalmi*. Ingenious indigenous water technologies are practiced throughout the country, including hand dug underground water channel systems called *karez*. These carry water for many miles from the base of mountains to fields on the plains.

Agriculture and animal husbandry engage about 60 percent of the workforce and all producers, whether nomads or farmers, are tied to a market economy. In addition, the industries that began to develop after the 1930s and later in the 1960s were largely based on agricultural and pastoral products. During the war, the improved road system that was to facilitate access to markets was destroyed and the industrial complexes were stripped of machinery.

Rural-urban migration increased measurably as the road system improved and industrial complexes near cities proliferated. Urban expansion brought in new architectural styles and building materials; prefab cement apartment blocks required adjustments in living styles. Still, despite monumental jumps in urban populations nowhere were slums evident.

FAMILY

Although variations may exist between ethnic groups and those practicing different modes of subsistence, the family remains the single most important institution in Afghan society.
Characteristically, the Afghan family is endogamous (with parallel and cross-cousin marriages preferred), patriarchal (authority vested in male elders), patrilineal (inheritance through the male line), and patrilocal (girl moves to husband's place of residence on marriage). Polygyny (multiple wives) is permitted, but is no longer so widely practiced.

Within families there is a tendency toward respect for age, male or female, reverence for motherhood, eagerness for children, especially sons, and avoidance of divorce. Rigorously honored ideals emphasizing family cohesiveness through extended kinship networks endow the family with its primary function as a support system.

The extended family, the major economic and social unit in the society, replaces government because of the absence of an adequate nation-wide service infrastructure. Child socialization takes place within the family because of deficiencies in the education system. Thus, individual social, economic and political rights and obligations are found within the family which guarantees security to each man and woman, from birth to death.

The strength of this sense of family solidarity has been amply evident throughout the past years of disruption. Although families may be split and now reside on separate continents a world apart, those that are more affluent regularly send remittances to less fortunate family members. Many urban Afghan refugee families in Pakistan would otherwise be totally destitute. Similarly, newly arrived refugees always find shelter with families already established in Pakistan. At times, single family living spaces will be stretched to accommodate up to twenty new persons because family members cannot be turned away. Similar obligations extend to finding employment for relatives. This at times leads to the blatant nepotism which plagues the aid assistance network in Pakistan.

This is not to say that no tensions exist within the extended family system. Fierce competition over authority, inheritance, and individual aspirations do develop. The violent enmity that rises between cousins, for example, particularly over the selection of brides, is so often present that it has become a favorite theme of countless songs and folktales.

In Afghanistan extended families are characterized by residential unity be it in a valley, a village or a single compound. Extended family households may contain three to four generations including the male head of family and his wife, his brothers, several sons and their families, cousins with their families, as well as all unmarried and widowed females. Nuclear family households geographically grouped within extended family settings are also common. These will frequently accommodate elderly grandparents and single or widowed aunts. No matter how they may be spaced, these multigenerational units practice close economic cooperation and come together on all life-crisis occasions. This permits cohesive in-group solidarity to be maintained.

The core of the family consists of the mother-in-law, the daughters-in-law and daughters, with the senior woman reigning at the top of the power hierarchy within the household. In families with plural wives, each wife has her own room, with her own belongings and furnishings; sometimes her own cooking space is provided. The courtyard provides space for joint household activities and entertainment.

Relations between co-wives can be amiable, sister-like and mutually supportive in sharing household chores and in securing favorable attention from the husband, but relations can also be stormy and many men hesitate to take a second wife because of the fierce battles that can erupt. Some co-wives resort to magic to ease household tensions by purchasing a variety of amulets and charms, including dried hoopoe heads and wolf claws which are believed to guarantee loving attention from husbands, peace with mothers-in-law and sweet tempers all around.

The practice of taking more than one wife became less and less prevalent over the past few decades. Few men could afford to do so. Barrenness and a failure to produce sons are common reasons for its continuation. Barrenness is a frightening social stigma, not only for wives but for her family as well. Most men feel obliged to rectify the situation, but because divorce is so repugnant the option of a second wife is preferred by all.

In other cases, multiple wives are taken in order to fulfill familial obligations to provide unmarried kin or young widows with a home and security. Although the institution of the levirate in which a widow is married, with or without her consent, to a member of her deceased husband's family is explicitly forbidden in the Quran, it functions traditionally to stabilize family identification and ensure economic security. By the 1960s the levirate had all but ceased to function in many areas, but it was increasingly employed after 1978 because of the unprecedented number of war widows. The vulnerability of widows too young to have established a commanding status in the family hierarchy is more frequently addressed through the levirate today than in pre-exodus Afghanistan.

While male authority in the family is paramount in all groups, some important differences in male-female interrelations can be noted within rural and urban environments. In the rural areas interrelated responsibilities between men and women establish a bond of partnership that builds mutual respect. Carpet making is but one example. The men herd and sheer the sheep, the women spin the wool, the men dye the wool, the women weave the carpet, and the men market the product. One highly important family activity performed by rural women that is often overlooked is their management of family food supplies. A women, often an elderly member of the household, receives the household's supply of grain following the harvest. She must make sure that this supply of the family's basic food staple is apportioned correctly over the year until the next harvest comes in. Otherwise the family must go into debt, or starve. Household management and responsibility for the upbringing of children thus give rural women considerable authority in their domestic sphere.

By contrast, in traditional urban lower and middle class homes men daily leave the house to work at jobs with which women are not involved and about which they have little knowledge or interest. These women are consequently more rigidly relegated to purely domestic duties of serving husbands and caring for children. Remarkable changes took place among middle class and elite families after 1959 when the government supported the voluntary end to seclusion for women. Women sought education and moved into the public sphere in ever increasing numbers. Nevertheless, working women are still expected to socialize within the family, not with their colleagues at work.

The innate belief in male superiority provides an ideological basis for the acceptance of male control over families. Socially circumscribed and male determined roles open to women are believed necessary to maintain social order, and when women do not appear to be controlled in traditional ways, as, for example, when they take up unusual public career or behavioral roles, this is taken as a danger sign heralding social disintegration. Life crisis decisions about education, careers and marriage are, therefore, made by male family members.

Embodied in the acceptance of the male right to control decisions on female behavior is the dual concept of male prestige and family honor. Any evidence of independent female action is regarded as evidence of lost male control and results in ostracism, which adversely affects the entire family's standing within the community. Community pressures thus make women dependent on men, even among modernized urban families. On the other hand, since the construction of family and male reputations, notably their much valued honour, depends upon the good behavior of women,

women derive a certain amount of leverage within family relationships from their ability to damage family prestige through subtle nonconformist behavior, such as simply failing to provide adequate hospitality, or a lack of rectitude within the home.

Afghan society places much emphasis on hospitality and the rules of etiquette that distinguish good behavior toward guests. By disregarding social niceties a person diminishes the reputation of both the immediate family and the extended family or group. Conversely, families gain respect, maintain status and enhance their standing in the community through exemplary behavior.

Since the family is so central to the lives of men, women and children, and since women's roles are pivotal to family well-being, the selection of mates is of prime concern. The preferred mate is a close relative or at least within a related lineage; the ideal being the father's brother's daughter, or first cousin, although this is not always feasible. In reality the process is far more complicated and involves a multiplicity of considerations, including strengthening group solidarity, sustaining social order, confirming social status, enhancing wealth and power or economic and political standing, increasing control over resources, resolving disputes, and compensating for injury and death.

Within this complicated web governing marriage negotiations, other factors must also be taken into account such as sectarian membership, ethnic group, family status, kin relationships, and economic benefits. The bride's skills, industriousness and temperament is also considered and, with all, the happiness and welfare of the girl is often not neglected.

Although endogamous marriage is prevalent in all groups, marriage between ethnic groups have always occurred. Over the past few decades these have increased because large populations have settled outside their ancestral areas, communication networks have improved and industrial complexes have drawn workers from many areas. In addition, political and economic changes occasioned by these developments shifted the balance of various types of productive resources and this led to forging marital links

135

between unrelated and previously unconnected groups for benefits other than expressions of status.

Except in cases in which the institution of marriage is manipulated for political and economic purposes, female family members initiate the elaborate process of betrothal through their own women's networks. Men are generally not involved in the initial stages although sometimes a son will elicit the support of his mother; sometimes a brother will bring about a match for his sister with one of his friends, or even a young man she has observed from the rooftop of her home. Brother-sister bonds are very strong.

Men enter the process in order to set the financial agreements before the engagement is announced. These entail the transfer of money, property or livestock from the groom's family to the bride's family. The large sums frequently demanded should not be seen only as evidence of avaricious fathers. Brides gain status according to the value set for them; too meager sums devalue both father and bride in the eyes of their community. Islam does not prescribe such a brideprice, but does enjoin the giving of *mahr* in the form of money or property for the personal use of the bride so that her financial welfare may be ensured in the event of divorce. Islamic law does not include the concept of alimony.

In many cases, however, the bride fails to receive her legitimate portion of the marriage settlement. This causes friction, and cases concerning inheritance are frequently brought before the urban family courts, to which rural women seldom have access. In addition, because exorbitant sums are often demanded, many men are unable to marry until they are older. Very young girls, therefore, are frequently married to much older men. As a result young widowhood is common, giving rise to the practice of the levirate described above. Under normal circumstances, however, girls are married while in their teens to boys in their mid-twenties. Cases of child marriage, however, are not unknown .

Every marriage entails two exchanges. The dowry brought by the bride to her husband's home normally equals the value of the brideprice. It includes clothing, bedding and household utensils which are expected to last the couple for fifteen years. Most importantly, the quality of the dowry often influences the treatment and status accorded the bride on her arrival at her husband's home. A majority of the items are made by the girl, in cooperation with her female relatives and friends. The preparation of the bridal hope chest, therefore, constitutes a crucial female activity in every home. The trousseau of embroidered, woven and tailored items is important to the prestige of both families and must be as impressive as possible.

The ratio of inheritance is two to one in favor of males; a wife receives one-third of her son's shares. In practice, women are often denied their rightful inheritance, again causing tensions not only within nuclear families, but among kin groups of the wife as well.

Various tribal and ethnic groups follow practices which are not strictly consistent with Islamic law. Past governments have sought to institutionalize social reforms pertaining to the family for over one hundred years. Using the dictates of Islam, Afghan monarchs since Amir Abdur Rahman (1880-1901) have decreed and legislated against child marriages, forced marriages, the levirate and exorbitant brideprices. They upheld hereditary rights of women, authorized women to receive the *mahr* for their personal use, and supported the right of women to seek divorce under certain circumstances such as non-support, maltreatment and impotency.

Subsequent constitutions while guaranteeing equal rights to men and women tended to avoid specific reference to women. The Penal Code of 1976 and Civil Law of 1977, however, contained familiar articles outlawing child marriage, forced marriage and abandonment but at the same time combined them with elements of customary laws favorable to male dominance and prejudicial to women in matters of divorce, child custody, adultery and the defence of male honour. A Special Court for Family Affairs opened in 1975 in which female judges participated, but such legal documents were scarcely heeded by the majority of the population because they were seen to interfere with family prerogatives in matters seen to be the provenance of Islam and therefore beyond the competence of secular law.

The leftist Democratic Republic of Afghanistan which came to power on 27 April 1978, issued Decree No. 7 with the expressed purpose of ensuring "equal rights of women with men and ... removing the unjust patriarchal feudalistic relations between husband and wife for the consolidation of sincere family ties." This simplistic decree, like earlier pronouncements, forbade child marriage, forced marriages and exorbitant brideprices. The DRA's social reforms were viewed as a threat to cherished cultural values and an intolerable intrusion into the closely- knit, family-based society and consequently met with early dissent. Rhetoric urging children to defy family restraints and inform on parents was repugnant. Encroachments on family decision-making concerning the conduct of female members was intolerable. The establishment of day-care centers usurped the family's paramount role in child socialization and sending young children to the Soviet Union for education was regarded as a particularly barbarous weapon designed to break up the family through the replacement of stable traditional relationships with fragmented, individualized interactions. As the massive flow of refugees into Pakistan began in 1979, many cited the assault on the integrity of their families as a major reason for their flight.

Decree No. 7 was the first DRA regulation to be eliminated by The Islamic State of Afghanistan on its assumption of power in 1992. To the Taliban, all past legislation touching upon women and the family threatened to undermine the society's values. As such they are anathema. Under the Taliban the sanctity of the family, with secluded women at its core, is a paramount requisite in their crusade to establish a fully Islamic society.

[RESERVED]

GENDER ROLES

Afghan society is consistent in its attitudes toward the underlying principles of gender. It is the application of these principles that varies from group to group; and there is a wide range of standards set for accepted female behavior, as well as differences in male attitudes toward correct treatment of women. Contradictions arise between traditional customary practices, many of which impinge on the rights of women and are alien to the spirit of Islam, the other functioning canon which emphasizes equality, justice, education and community service for both men and women. Further, the dictates of Islam are themselves subject to diverse interpretation among reformists, Islamists and ultraconservatives. Debates between these groups can be highly volatile.

Gender reform was central to the contentious issues which brought about the fall of King Amanullah in 1929. In 1959, the male-oriented government of Prime Minister Daud Khan supported the voluntary removal of the veil and the end of seclusion for women. The 1964 Constitution automatically enfranchised women and guaranteed them the right to education and freedom to work.

For thirty years after 1959 growing numbers of women, most from urban backgrounds, functioned in the public arena with poise and dignity, with no loss of honor to themselves or to their families, and with much credit to the nation. Nevertheless, family pressures, traditional attitudes and religious opposition continued to impose constraints which limited the degree to which women could find self-expression and control their lives.

Except in Kabul where women under the PDPA were encouraged to assume more assertive public roles, this evolutionary movement came to a halt in 1978. Conservative mujahidin leaders waging a *jihad* (struggle) against foreign encroachment, both military and ideological, were imbued with the belief that sexual anarchy would result if women continued to move freely in public;

and that society would fall into ruin as a result. These attitudes have intensified under the Taliban. Mostly rural Pushtun from strongly patriarchal backgrounds, the Taliban project ultraconservative interpretations of Islam and apply customary practices as societal ideals. In 1996, gender issues are again at the center of heated deba e.

All agree that differences between men and women exist and are best preserved through recognized standards of behavior. None dispute the centrality of women in the society. Respect for women is a notable characteristic and few wish to destroy this esteemed status, nor deny what Islam enjoins or Afghan culture values. The argument rages over definitions of precisely what constitutes honorable behavior for women in terms of modern realities, especially in the light of today's monumental reconstruction needs which demand full participation from every Afghan citizen.

The current zealous need to protect women's morality stems from the fact that Afghan society regards women as the perpetuators of the ideals of the society. As such they symbolize honor -- of family, community and nation -- and must be controlled as well as protected so as to maintain moral purity. By imposing strict restraints directly on women, the society's most sensitive component symbolizing male honor, authorities convey their intent to subordinate personal autonomy and thereby strengthen the impression that they are capable of exercising control over all aspects of social behavior, male and female.

The practice of *purdah*, seclusion, (Persian, literally meaning curtain), including veiling, is the most visible manifestation of this attitude. This concept includes an insistence on separate spaces for men and women and proscriptions against interactions between the sexes outside the *mahrammat* (acceptable male guardians such as father, brother son and any other male with whom a women may not marry). These restrictions severely limit women's activities, including access to education and employment outside the home. Many are largely confined to their homes.

Such restrictions are deemed necessary by conservative males because they consider women socially immature, with less moral control and physical restraint; women's hypersexuality precludes responsible behavior. Consequently, women are untrustworthy and must be kept behind the curtain so as not to disrupt the social order. The need for their isolation therefore is paramount.

Afghan women view their sexuality more positively and question male maturity and self-control. In reality the differences between private and public behavior are significant. In private, there is a noticeable sharing of ideas and responsibilities and in many households individual charisma and strength of character surmounts conventional subordinate roles. Even moral misconduct can be largely overlooked until it becomes a matter of public knowledge. Then punishment must be severe for male and family honor must be vindicated. It is the public image that counts.As a result, urban women are models of reticence in public and rural women appear properly submissive.

That a family's social position depends on the public behavior of its female members is a guiding reality. Stepping outside prescribed roles and behavioral norms in public results in moral condemnation and social ostracism. It is the dictates of society that place a burden on both men and women to conform.

Under such circumstances gender roles necessarily follow defined paths. Male prerogatives reside in family economic welfare, politics, and relationships with outsiders; within the family they are expected to be disciplinarians and providers for aged parents. Female roles stress motherhood, child socialization and family nurturing. Even among professional career women, family responsibilities remain a top priority. Thus women's self-perception of their roles, among the majority, urban and rural, contributes to the perpetuation of patriarchal values.

Within the vast store of Afghan folktales covering religion, history and moral values, many reinforce the values governing male and female behavior. They illustrate what can or cannot be done, describe rewards and punishments, and define ideal personality types. Thus they serve to perpetuate the existing gender order and through example make it psychologically satisfying.

The status and power of a girl increases as she moves from child to bride to mother to grandmother. A successful marriage with many sons is the principal goal of Afghan women, wholeheartedly shared by Afghan men. Women's nurturing roles are also crucial. This does not mean that women are confined to domestic roles. The stereotyping of Afghan women as chattel living lives of unremitting labor, valued by men solely for sexual pleasure and reproductive services is patently false.

Women's work varies from group to group. Among most settled rural families, women participate in agricultural work only during light harvesting periods, and are responsible for the production of milk products. Some specialize in handicrafts such as carpet and felt making. In contrast, Nuristani women plow the fields while the men herd the flocks and process the dairy products. Nomadic women care for young lambs and kids and make a wide variety of dairy products, for sale as well as family use. They spin the wool sheered by men and weave the fabric from which their tents are made. Felt-making for yurt coverings and household rugs ia also a female activity. When on the move, it is the women who put up and take down the tents. The variations are endless.

Although statistics indicate that by 1978 women were joining the workforce in increasing numbers, only about eight percent of the female population received an income. Most of these women lived in urban centers, and the majority were professionals, technicians and administrators employed by the government which continued its strong support. A majority worked in health and education, the two sectors considered most appropriate for women as they are extensions of traditional women's roles. Others worked in the police, the army, and with the airlines; in government textile, ceramic, food processing and prefab construction factories. A few worked in private industry; a few were self-employed.

The current revival of conservative attitudes toward appropriate extradomestic roles for women and the criticism of women's visibility in public has largely impacted these professional women.

144

Islamic texts do not delineate roles for women. What they imply is open to interpretation. What they command is equality and justice guaranteeing that women be treated as in no way lesser than men. Educated Afghan women are standing fast in their determination to find ways in which they may participate in the nation's reconstruction according to their interpretations of Islam's tenets. This is a powerful challenge now facing the society.

However, the foreign aid community would do well to examine carefully their recent aggressive campaign to assure rights for Afghan women in education and employment. The Afghan community is already sharply divided over whether assistance to boys' education should be discontinued because there is a ban on education for girls. Family harmony must certainly be undermined when women are favored over men in a declining job market.

RELIGION

Islam is one of the few commonalities in Afghan society despite the existence of sectarian differences and variations in Quranic and legal interpretations. It faces no competition from other religions as only scattered minorities of Hindus and Sikhs, who came originally as traders from India, and Jews, lived in urban centers. By 1985 virtually all Jews had emigrated.

In their war of liberation against the Soviet Union, resistance groups striving for a pan-Afghan constituency appealed to Afghans on the basis of their Muslim identity. The term used for the resistance fighters, mujahidin, translates as "those waging jihad." Jihad, meaning to strive or to struggle to follow God's will, both within oneself and in the defense of Islam, is an obligation incumbent on all Muslims.

Early Development of Islam

In AD 570 Mohammad ibn Abdullah was born into the family of a caravan merchant belonging to the Hashimite branch of the ruling Quraysh tribe that lived in the prosperous Arabian town of Mecca. In AD 610, at the age of forty, Mohammad began to receive the first of a series of revelations from God which were transmitted to him through the angel Gabriel over a period of 22 years. These directives of moral principles are contained in the Quran (The Recitation), the sacred scripture of Islam.

The Prophet Mohammad preached against socioeconomic inequities and denounced polytheism with its thriving pilgrimage business centered around the Kaaba shrine and numerous religious sites in the vicinity of Mecca. His vigorous reform messages challenged the powerful ruling establishment, threatened their economic and political interests and eventually earned him their bitter enmity.

Forced to leave Mecca in 622, he moved with a group of followers to the town of Yathrib, later called Medina. Here he established a Muslim community-state, consolidating both temporal and spiritual leadership in his person. The migration to Medina is known as the *hijra* and the creation of a Muslim community (*ummah*) marks the beginning of the Islamic era. The Muslim calendar, based on a 354-day lunar year, begins in AD 622. From Medina, the Prophet Mohammad fought a series of successful battles and returned to Mecca in triumph in AD 630, shortly before his death in 632.

After the Prophet Mohammad's death, the leaders of the Muslim community chose as his successor or *caliph*, Abu Bakr, who was one of the Prophet's earliest followers as well as the father of Aisha, the youngest and most beautiful of the Prophet's wives. There were those, however, who favored Ali, the Prophet's cousin and husband of his daughter Fatima. These supporters of Ali were known as Shiat-u-Ali (Party of Ali), later to be called Shia. Ali eventually succeeded as the fourth caliph in AD 656, but this led to civil war in 661 during which Ali was assassinated. Ali's son Husayn led a second rebellion in 680 during which he was killed at the Battle of Karbala which is commemorated by the Shia each year on the tenth of Muharram. Husayn's death marks the division of Islam into Sunni and Shia, ending the period in which the entire Islamic community recognized a single caliph.

Sunni and Shia Islam

The historical divide of Islam into Sunni, or so-called orthodox Islam, and Shia, was caused more by political dispute over successors than doctrinal differences, although differences gradually assumed theological and metaphysical overtones. Despite the split, within centuries Islam reached far into Africa, eastward to the Indian subcontinent and southeast Asia, as well as northward into Central Asia. This expansion was accomplished by traders and missionaries as much as by conquest.

Sunni constitute 85 percent of the world's Muslims; Shia about 15 percent. Each division has four major Shariah or schools of theological law. The Sunni: Hanafi, dominant in the Arab Middle East, India, Pakistan and Afghanistan; Maleki, in north, central and west Africa and Egypt; Shafii, in east Africa, Indonesia and southeast Asia; Hanbali, in Saudi Arabia. The Shia: Ithna Ashariya or Imami, the state religion in Iran, dominant in Iraq and also found in Afghanistan; Nizari Ismaili, present throughout the Muslim world, including Afghanistan, led by the Aga Khan; Zaidiya, in Yemen; Mutazila, in Syria and Lebanon.

Sufism

The growth of Sufism (from *suf*, Arabic for wool; possibly referring to woolen robes worn by early ascetics) was another important development in the history of Islam. The great Sufi orders or brotherhoods (*tariqa*) were first established in the twelfth century by scholars disillusioned in their search for Truth through the intellectual application of the austere practices advocated by the various schools of Islamic doctrine. A belief in the oneness of man with God is central to Sufism. Sufis seek to achieve a personal communion with God during mystic moments of union brought about by various methods, including meditation, recitation of sacred phrases, breathing exercises, dancing, hymn singing, music, and physical gyrations.

Sufi religious life centers around a learned religious leader or spiritual guide referred to as *shaykh* (in Persian, *pir*) whose mystical teachings guide students (*murids*) along the path (*tariqa*) that leads each to the ecstacy of his own moment of intimacy with God. Relationships between the master and disciple are very close. Many famous Sufi shaykh attracted large bodies of followers, and the sites of their brotherhoods became not only renowned spiritual institutions, but also popular social and cultural community centers providing medical, educational, and welfare services, including soup kitchens for the poor and hungry. These centers oftentimes amassed considerable wealth from gifts from pilgrims and from endowments (*awaqf*, singular, *waqf*), an important institution providing community social services. With wealth they acquired social and political power. This building of a sense of an alternative community within Sufism threatened the status of established religious authorities (*ulama*), undermining their institutionalized perceptions of an universal, unified Islamic community (*ummah*) following the *Shariah*, the "straight path" of Islamic law. The orthodox ulama initially declared Sufism heretical, but over time came to tolerate it as long as its adherents abided by Islamic laws.

Sufi practices are found today among both Sunni and Shia communities, although it tends to be more widespread among Sunnis, perhaps because Shia attach great value to the intercession of saints and most Shia embrace mysticism and encourage emotional responses to God and to Shia martyrs, especially those connected with the tragedy of Karbala which is commemorated on Ashura, the 10th day of Moharram, when dramatic recitations, passion plays (*taziya*) and street processions, which include self-flagellation, take place.

Sufis describe their personal experiences in a vast variety of poetic expression. The poetry of the Sufis is considered the best in the Persian language, and among the most notable of all poetic styles. Particularly honored are Sadi and Hafiz of Shiraz in Iran, and Baydil from the Persian-speaking Moghal court of Delhi. Universally acclaimed Afghan Sufi poets include Ansari (eleventh century) and Jami (fifteenth century) of Herat, Sanayi of Ghazni (twelfth century) , and Rumi of Balkh (thirteenth century), the founder of the order of whirling dervishes, whose *Mathnawi* is considered by many to be the greatest poem ever written in Persian.

Tenets of Islam

Islam means surrender or submission to the will of God; one who submits is a MuslimThe basic creed or profession of faith, the *shahadah*, succinctly states: "There is no god but Allah (God), and Mohammad is His Prophet/Messenger." Mohammad is the "seal of the prophets"; his revelation is believed to complete for all time the series of revelations received by Jews and Christians.

After the Prophet's death, his followers compiled those of his words regarded as coming directly and literally from God. This became the Quran, the holy scripture of Islam. The precedent of the Prophet's personal deeds and behavior were set forth in the *Sunna* as a supplement extending the Quran. Other sayings and teachings recalled by those who had known him during his lifetime are known as *Hadith*. Together, the Quran, the Sunnah and the Hadith form a comprehensive guide to the spiritual, ethical, and social conduct of life. Islamic jurisprudence, the *Shariah*, which is based on these sources, is a system of ethics regulating conduct.

Thus Islam is a legalistic religion with sets of God-given laws that are applied to all aspects of everyday life. Historically, Islam recognizes no distinction between religious and temporal spheres of life for all human behavior is expected to comply with God's will. It draws no distinction between the religious and the secular nor differentiates between religious and secular law. Therefore there is no concept of the separation of church and state.

The *Shariah*, along with commentaries (*tafsir*) on the Quran and Hadith, developed primarily through the accretion of precedent and interpretations by various learned judges and scholars (*ulama*) attempting to divine the will of Allah through juristic analogical reasoning (*qiyas*) and consensus (*ijma*). By the tenth and eleventh centuries, these legal opinions had hardened into rigid authoritative doctrine, and the right to exercise independent reasoned interpretation (*ijtihad*) was effectively denied. This severely limited flexibility in Sunni Islamic law. In contrast, Shia Islam tended not to curb the use of *ijtihad* to such an extent.

Sunni communities have no clerical hierarchy: each individual stands in a personal relationship to God needing no intermediary. Any adult versed in the form of prayer is entitled to lead prayers. Men who lead prayers preach sermons, and interpret the law do so by virtue of their superior knowledge and scholarship rather than because of any special powers or prerogatives conferred by ordination. Among the Shia, on the other hand, a highly structured· hierarchy of divinely inspired religio-political leaders exists. The Imam who must be directly descended from the Prophet Mohammad and Ali is invested as the final authoritative interpreter of God's will as formulated by Islamic law.

Every individual is responsible for carrying out the duties and rituals commonly referred to as the Five Pillars of Islam. These include the recitation of the creed (*shahadah*), daily prayer (*salat, namaz* in Afghanistan), almsgiving (*zakat*), fasting (*sawm, ruzah* in Afghanistan), and pilgrimage (*hajj*).

The *muezzin* intones the call to prayer to the entire community five times a day, at day-break, midday, mid-afternoon, sunset and nightfall. Ritual ablutions of purification proceed prayers. Prescribed body movements, including genuflections and prostrations, accompany the prayers, which the worshiper recites while facing toward Mecca, the holy center of Islam where the Kaaba has remained sacred since the polytheistic idols were destroyed following the conquest of Mecca in AD 630. Prayers may be performed wherever a person may be at the required time, but congregational prayers in the central mosque on Friday are usual. Friday noon prayers provide the occasion for weekly sermons by religious leaders. In numbers of Muslim societies, women may also worship at mosques where they are provided segregated areas, although most prefer to pray at home.

Daily prayers consist of specified prayers, including the opening verse and other passages from the Quran. At the end, the *shahadah* is recited. Prayers seeking aid or guidance in personal difficulties must be offered separately.

152

Zakat or almsgiving fulfills the individual's obligation towards his shared responsibility for the welfare of the community. Alms may be given individually; in some cases zakat is collected for distribution by governments.

The ninth month of the Muslim calendar is Ramadan (in Arabic) a period of obligatory fasting that commemorates the Prophet Mohammad's receipt of God's revelation, the Quran. Fasting is an act of self-discipline that leads to piety and expresses submission and commitment to God. By underscoring the equality of all Muslims, fasting strengthens a sense of community. During Ramadan, all but the sick, weak, pregnant or nursing women, soldiers on duty, travelers on necessary journeys, and young children are enjoined from eating, drinking, sexual activity, or smoking from sunrise to sunset. Official work hours often are shortened during this period.

Because the lunar calendar is eleven days shorter than the solar calendar, Ramadan revolves through the seasons over the years. When Ramadan falls in the summertime, a fast imposes considerable hardship on those who must do physical work. Id al Fitr, a three-day feast and holiday, ends the month of Ramadan and is the occasion for new clothes and much visiting between family members.

Ramadan is followed by the beginning of the *hajj* pilgrimage season during the twelfth month of the lunar calendar. At least once in their lifetime both men and women should, if economically able, make the hajj to the holy city of Mecca where special rites are focused on the Kaaba and nearby sites associated with the Prophet Ibrahim (Abraham) and his son Ismail. Pilgrims, dressed in two white, seamless pieces of cloth (*ihram*), perform various traditional rites expressing unity and harmony with the worldwide Muslim community (*ummah*) by affirming obedience to God and their intent to lead a righteous life following the path directed by God. Returning pilgrims are entitled to use the honorific "hajji" and enjoy a respected status in their communities. Id al Adha, the feast of sacrifice, marks the end of the hajj month. The sacrificial meat is often shared with neighbors and the needy.

The permanent struggle for the triumph of God's word on earth, *jihad*, represents an additional duty. This concept is often taken to mean holy war, but in its basic sense it encompasses the efforts made by individuals to live a virtuous life overcoming all forms of evil so as to follow Islam.

Aside from specific duties, Islam imposes a code of ethical conduct encouraging generosity, fairness, honesty, tolerance, respect and service for the benefit of the common welfare of the *ummah*. It forbids the shedding of human blood, thieving and lying. It also gives explicit guidance on proper family relations and forbids adultery, gambling, usury, and the consumption of carrion, blood, pork, and alcohol.

Islamic Expression in Afghanistan

Arab armies carrying the banner of Islam reached the Afghan area in AD 642. On the western periphery, the princes of Herat and Seistan gave way to rule by Arab governors, but in the east cities submitted only to rise in revolt and the hastily converted returned to their old beliefs once the armies passed. Later, in the 9th century, Yaqub ibn Layth Saffari, founder of the local Saffarid dynasty in the Seistan, swept through the Afghan area conquering in the name of Islam; in the north the Islamic dynasty of the Samanids ruling from Bokhara took Balkh in AD 900 and extended their realm as far as Kandahar. Meanwhile a Turkish slave general who had been dismissed by the Samanids conquered Ghazni. A successor, the great Sultan Mahmud of Ghazni (998-1030), conducted numerous iconoclastic campaigns into India and returned laden with rich booty. Ghazni, until then an insignificant fort-town, became one of the most brilliant capitals of the Islamic world.

Today, approximately 99 percent of Afghans are Muslims. Eighty-five percent are Sunni of the Hanafi School; the rest are

Shia, the majority of whom are Imami along with smaller numbers of Ismailis. There is also a strong influence of Sufism among both Sunni and Shia communities.

Sunnis of the Hanafi School

The Hanafi school of Islamic jurisprudence was founded by Abu Hanifa, one of the earliest Muslim scholar-interpreters to seek new ways of applying Islamic tenets to everyday life. He died in Iraq in AD 767. Abu Hanifa's interpretation of Muslim law was extremely tolerant of differences within Muslim communities. He also separated belief from practice, elevating belief over practice. Sunni are found throughout Afghanistan.

Ithna Ashariya (Twelver or Imami) Shia

Religious succession is basic to Shia/Sunni differences, and also divides the Shia. The two major Shia communities in Afghanistan are the Ithna Ashariya or Twelvers, also called Imami, and the Ismaili, sometimes called the Seveners. The Imami Shia recognize twelve successive Imams, beginning with Ali and ending in AD 874 with the disappearance of the twelfth who will return as a messianic figure at the end of the world.

The most numerous Imami Shia groups in Afghanistan are the Imami Hazara living in the Hazarajat of central Afghanistan, and the Imami Farsiwan of Herat Province. Mixtures occur in certain areas such as Bamiyan Province where Sunni, Imami and Ismaili may be found. Imami Shia are also found in urban centers such as Kabul, Kandahar, Ghazni, and Mazar-i-Sharif where numbers of Qizilbash and Hazara reside. Urban Shia are successful small business entrepreneurs; many gained from the development of education that began in the 1950s.

The political involvement of Shia communities grew

dramatically during the politicized era during and following the Soviet invasion. Politically aware Shia students formed the hard core of the Afghan Maoist movement of the 1960s and early 1970s After 1978, Shia mujahidin groups in the Hazarajat, although frequently at odds with one another, were active in the jihad and subsequently in the fighting for the control of Kabul. During the political maneuvering leading up to the establishment of The Islamic State of Afghanistan in 1992, the Shia groups unsuccessfully negotiated for more equitable, consequential political and social roles. This heightened profile created a backlash among some Sunni groups, notably those associated with the Hezb-i Islami of Mawlawi Yunus Khalis and the Ittihad-i-Islam of Professor Abd al-Rabb al-Rasul Sayyaf. Violent sectarian confrontations took place, particularly in and around Kabul.

Ismailis

The Ismaili Shia are also known as Seveners because in the eighth century their leaders rejected the heir designated by the sixth Imam, Jafar al Sadiq (d.765), whom the Imami accepted. The new group instead chose to recognize Jafar's eldest son, Ismail, as the seventh Imam and the Shia community split into two branches.

Ismaili communities in Afghanistan are less populous than the Imami who consider the Ismailis heretical. They are found primarily in and near the eastern Hazarajat, in the Baghlan area north of the Hindu Kush, among the mountain Tajik of Badakhshan, and amongst the Wakhi in the Wakhan Corridor.

Many Ismaili believe the line of Imam ceased when Ismail died before his father in AD 760; others believe he did not die but remains in seclusion and will return at the end of the world. Ismaili beliefs are complex and syncretic, combining elements from the philosophies of Plotinus, Pythagoras, Aristotle, gnosticism, and the Manichaeans, as well as components of Judaism, Christianity, and Eastern religions. Ismaili conceptions of the Imamat differ greatly from those of other Muslims and their tenets are unique. Their

156

beliefs about the creation of the world are idiosyncratic, as is their historical ecumenism, tolerance of religious differences, and religious hierarchy. There is a division of theology into exoteric (including the conservative *Shariah*) and esoteric (including the mystical exegesis of the Quran which leads to *haqiqa*, the ultimate realty). These beliefs and practices are veiled in secrecy and Ismaili place particular emphasis on *taqiya* meaning to shield or guard, the practice that permits the believer to deny publicly his Shia membership for self-protection, as long as he continues to believe and worship in private. *Taqiya* is permissible in most Shia, and some Sunni, sects.

Ismailis in Afghanistan are generally regarded with suspicion by other ethnic groups and for the most part their economic status is very poor. Although Ismaili in other areas such as the northern areas of Pakistan operate well-organized social welfare programs including schools, hospitals and cooperatives, little has been done among Afghan Ismaili communities.

Considered less zealous than other Afghan Muslims, Ismaili are seen to follow their leaders uncritically. The *pir* or leader of Afghan Ismailis comes from the Sayyid family of Kayan, located near Doshi, a small town at the northern foot of the Salang Pass, in western Baghlan Province. During the Soviet-Afghan War this family acquired considerable political power.

Sufis

Sufism has considerable influence in Afghanistan, in both rural and urban settings, especially among the middle classes of larger villages, town and cities.

Three Sufi orders are prominent: the Naqshbandiya founded in Bokhara, the Qadiriya founded in Baghdad, and the Cheshtiya located at Chesht-i-Sharif east of Herat. Among the Naqshbani, Ahmad al Faruqi Kabuli, born north of Kabul, acquired renown for his teachings in India during the reign of the Moghul Emperor

Akbar in the sixteenth century. Sometime during the nineteenth century members of this family moved back to Kabul where they established a *madrassa* and a *khanaqah* in Shor Bazar which became a center of religious and political influence. Many Afghan Naqshbandi are linked with the Mujaddedi family. Sibghatullah Mujaddedi, leader of the *mujahidin* Jabha-i Nejat-i Melli party, became the head of this order when his predecessor, along with 79 male members of the family, were executed in Kabul by the Taraki-Amin government in January 1979. He served for two months as the first acting president of the Islamic State of Afghanistan established in April 1992.

Hazrat Naqib Sahib, father of Sayyid Ahmad Gailani Effendi, the present pir of the Qadiriya, established the family seat in Afghanistan on the outskirts of Jalalabad during the 1920s. Pir Ahmad Gailani is the leader of the *mujahidin* Mahaz-i Melli Islami party. The leadership of both the Naqshbandiya and Qadiriya orders derive from heredity rather than religious scholarship.

The Cheshtiya order was founded by Mawdid al-Cheshti who was born in the twelfth century and later taught in India. The Cheshtiya brotherhood, concentrated in the Hari Rud valley around Obe, Karukh and Chehst-i-Sharif, is very strong locally and maintains *madrasas* with fine libraries. Traditionally the Cheshtiya have kept aloof from politics, although they were effectively active during the resistance within their own organizations and in their own areas.

Herat and its environs has the largest number and greatest diversity of Sufi branches, many of which are connected with local tombs of *pir* (*ziarat*). Other Sufi groups are found all across the north, with important centers in Maimana, Faryab Province, and in Kunduz. The brotherhoods in Kabul and around Mazar-i-Sharif are mostly associated with the Naqshbandiya. The Qadiriya are found mainly among the eastern Pushtun of Wardak, Paktya and Ningrahar, including many Ghilzai nomadic groups. Other smaller groups are settled in Kandahar and in Shindand, Farah Province. The Cheshtiya are centered in the Hari Rud Valley. There are no formal Sufi orders among the Shia in the central Hazarajat, although some of the concepts are associated with Sayyids, descendants of the Prophet Mohammad, who are especially venerated among the Shia.

Afghanistan is unique in that there is little hostility between the *ulama* and the Sufi orders. Numbers of Sufi leaders are considered as *ulama*, and many *ulama* closely associate with Sufi brotherhoods. The general populace accords Sufis respect for their learning and for possessing *karamat*, the psychic spiritual power conferred upon them by God that enables pirs to perform acts of generosity and bestow blessings (*barakat*). Sufism therefore is an effective popular force. In addition, since Sufi leaders distance themselves from the mundane, they are at times turned to as more disinterested mediators in tribal disputes in preference to mullahs who are reputed to escalate minor secular issues into volatile confrontations couched in Islamic rhetoric.

Meaning and Practice

Islam represents a potentially unifying symbolic system which offsets the divisiveness that frequently rises from the existence of a deep pride in tribal loyalties and an abounding sense of personal and family honor found in multitribal and multiethnic societies such as Afghanistan.

Islam is a central, pervasive influence throughout Afghan society; religious observances punctuate the rythmn of each day and season. In addition to a central Friday mosque for weekly communal prayers which are not obligatory but generally attended, smaller community-maintained mosques stand at the center of villages, as well as town and city neighborhoods. Mosques serve not only as places of worship, but for a multitude of functions, including shelter for guests, places to meet and gossip, the focus of social religious festivities and schools. Almost every Afghan has at one time during his youth studied at a mosque school; for many this is the only formal education they receive.

Because Islam is a total way of life and functions as a comprehensive code of social behavior regulating all human relationships, individual and family status depends on the proper observance of the society's value system based on concepts defined in Islam. These are characterized by honesty, frugality, generosity, virtuousness, piousness, fairness, truthfulness, tolerance and respect for others. To uphold family honor, elders also control the behavior of their children according to these same Islamic prescriptions. At times, even competitive relations between tribal or ethnic groups are expressed in terms claiming religious superiority. In short, Islam structures day-to-day interactions of all members of the community.

The religious establishment consists of several levels. Any Muslim can lead informal groups in prayer. Mullahs who officiate at mosques are normally appointed by the government after consultation with their communities and, although partially financed by the government, mullahs are largely dependent for their livelihood on community contributions including shelter and a portion of the harvest. Supposedly versed in the Quran, Sunnah, Hadith and Shariah, they must ensure that their communities are knowledgeable in the fundamentals of Islamic ritual and behavior. This qualifies them to arbitrate disputes over religious interpretation. Often they function as paid teachers responsible for religious education classes held in mosques where children learn basic moral values and correct ritual practices. Their role has additional social aspects for they officiate on the occasion of life crisis rituals associated with births, marriages and deaths.

But rural mullahs are not part of an institutionalized hierarchy of clergy. Most are part-time mullahs working also as farmers or craftsmen. Some are barely literate, or only slightly more educated than the people they serve. Often, but by no means always, they are men of minimal wealth and, because they depend for their livelihood on the community that appoints them, they have little authority even within their own social boundaries. They are often treated with scant respect and are the butt of a vast body of jokes making fun of their arrogance and ignorance. Yet their role as religious arbiters forces them to take positions on issues that have political ramifications and since mullahs often disagree with one another, pitting one community against the other, they are frequently perceived as disruptive elements within their communities.

Other religious figures include the *muezzin* who calls the congregation to prayer and the *khadim*, the mosque caretakers. *Qari* are experts at reciting the Quran; *hafiz* know it by heart. Hafiz are often blind and associated with brotherhoods at important shrines. *Qazi*, religious judges, are part of the government judicial system responsible for the application of *Shariah* laws.

Ulama is the term that describes the body of scholars who have acquired *ilm* or religious learning. As such they are seen as the transmitters of religious texts, doctrines and values, as well as interpreters of the *Shariah*. *Maulana* and *Mawlawi* are titles given to members of the ulama and religious dignitaries. Sayyids among both Sunni and Shia refer to descendants of the Prophet Mohammad who enjoy social and religious prestige throughout the Muslim world.

Within Sufi networks there are a host of religious personalities in addition to *pirs*. Among these are various types of mendicants such as *malangs* who renounce the impermanence of this world and embrace poverty in order to detach themselves from the chains of materialism so as to better realize the divine. Some malang attach themselves to, or swear loyalty to, a particular brotherhood, but others wander alone, often garbed in colorful creative clothing. Some, like *faqirs*, claim to have been given a Divine mission and miraculous powers. They eschew home, family and worldly goods, sleeping in mosques or graveyards, especially those attached to shrines of saints. In a culture where family and kin are basic to individual psychological and economic identity, anyone who voluntarily relinquishes these ties is considered to have been favored by God with a special mission. As a result, they are respectfully tolerated and often given alms.

Veneration of saints and shrines (*mazar, ziarat*) is notencouragedin Islam and is actively suppressed by some groups. Nevertheless, Afghanistan's landscape is liberally strewn with shrines honoring saints of all descriptions. Many of Afghanistan's oldest villages and towns grew up around shrines of considerable antiquity. Some are used as sanctuaries by fugitives.

Shrines vary in form from simple mounds of earth or stones marked by pennants to lavishly ornamented complexes surrounding a central domed tomb. These large establishments are controlled by prominent religious and secular leaders. Shrines may mark the final resting place of a fallen hero (*shahid*), a venerated religious teacher, a renowned Sufi poet, or relics, such as a hair of the Prophet Mohammad or a piece of his cloak (*khirqah*). A great many commemorate legends about the miraculous exploits of Ali, the first Imam of Shia Islam, believed to be buried at the nation's most elaborate shrine located in the heart of Mazar-i-Sharif, the Exalted Shrine. Hazrat Ali is revered throughout Afghanistan for his role as an intermediary in the face of tyranny.

Festive annual fairs celebrated at shrines attract thousands of pilgrims and bring together all sections of communities. Pilgrims also visit shrines to seek the intercession of the saint for special favors, be it a cure for illness or the birth of a son. Women are particularly devoted to activities associated with shrines. These visits may be short or last several days and many pilgrims carry away specially blessed curative and protective amulets (*tawiz*) to ward off the evil eye, assure loving relationships between husbands and wives and many other forms of solace.

Politicized Islam

Although Shariah courts existed in urban centers after Ahmad Shah Durrani established an Afghan state in 1747, the primary judicial basis for the society remained in the tribal code of the *Pushtunwali* until the end of the nineteenth century. Sporadic *fatwas* (formal legal opinions) were issued and occasional *jihads* were called not so much to advance Islamic ideology as to sanction the actions of specific individuals against their political opponents so that power might be consolidated.

The first systematic employment of Islam as an instrument for state-building was introduced by Amir Abdur Rahman (1880-1901) during his drive toward centralization. He decreed that all laws mustcomply with Islamic law and thus elevated the *Shariah* over customary laws embodied in the *Pushtunwali*. The *ulama* were enlisted to legitimize and sanction his state efforts as well as his central authority. This enhanced the religious community on the one hand, but as they were increasingly inducted into the bureaucracy as servants of the state, the religious leadership was ultimately weakened. Many economic privileges enjoyed by religious personalities and institutions were restructured within the framework of the state, the propagation of learning, once the sole prerogative of the ulama, was closely supervised, and the Amir became the supreme arbiter of justice.

His successors continued and expanded Amir Abdur Rahman's policies as they increased the momentum of secularization. Islam continued central to interactions, but the religious establishment remained essentially non-political, functioning as a moral rather than a political influence. Nevertheless, Islam asserted itself in times of national crisis. And, when the religious leadership considered themselves severely threatened, charismatic religious personalities periodically employed Islam to rally disparate groups in opposition to the state. They rose up on several occasions against King Amanullah (1919-929), for example, in protest against reforms they believed to be western intrusions inimical to

Islam.

Subsequent rulers, mindful of traditional attitudes antithetical to secularization were careful to underline the compatibility of Islam with modernization. Even so, and despite its pivotal position within the society which continued to draw no distinction between religion and state, the role of religion in state affairs continued to decline.

The 1931 Constitution made the Hanafi *Shariah* the state religion, while the 1964 Constitution simply prescribed that the state should conduct its religious ritual according to the Hanafi School. The 1977 Constitution, declared Islam the religion of Afghanistan, but made no mention that the state ritual should be Hanafi. The Penal Code (1976) and Civil Law (1977), covering the entire field of social justice, represent major attempts to cope with elements of secular law, based on, but superseded by other systems. Courts, for instance, were enjoined to consider cases first according to secular law, resorting to the BCShariah in areas where secular law did not exist. By 1978, the government of the Peoples Democratic Party of Afghanistan (PDPA) openly expressed its aversion to the religious establishment. This precipitated the fledgling Islamist Movement into a national revolt; Islam moved from its passive stance on the periphery to play an active role.

Politicized Islam in Afghanistan represents a break from Afghan traditions. The Islamist Movement originated in 1958 among faculties of Kabul University, particularly within the Faculty of Islamic Law which had been formed in 1952 with the announced purpose of raising the quality of religious teaching to accommodate modern science and technology. The founders were largely professors influenced by the Egyptian Muslim Brotherhood, a party formed in the 1930s that was dedicated to Islamic revivalism and social, economic, and political equity. Their objective is to come to terms with the modern world through the development of a political ideology based on Islam. The Afghan leaders, while indebted to many of these concepts, did not forge strong ties to similar movements in other countries.

164

The liberalization of government attitudes following the passage of the 1964 Constitution ushered in a period of intense activism among students at Kabul University. Professors and their students set up the Muslim Youth Organization (Sazmani Jawanani Musulman) in the mid-1960s at the same time that the leftists were also forming many parties. Initially communist students outnumbered the Muslim students, but by 1970 the Muslim Youth had gained a majority in student elections. Their membership was recruited from university faculties and from secondary schools in several cities such as Mazar-i-Sharif and Herat. These professors and students became the leaders of the Afghan Resistance in the 1980s.

With the takeover of government by the PDPA in April 1978, Islam became central to uniting the opposition against the communist ideology of the new rulers. As a politico-religious system, Islam is ideally suited to the needs of a diverse, unorganized, often mutually antagonistic citizenry wishing to forge a united front against a common enemy; and war permitted various groups within the mujahidin to put into effect competing concepts of organization.

The mujahidin leaders were charismatic figures with dyadic ties to followers. In many cases military and political leaders replaced the tribal leadership; at times the religious leadership was strengthened; often the religious combined with the political leadership. Followers selected their local leaders on the basis of personal choice and precedence among regions, sects, ethnic groups or tribes, but the major leaders rose to prominence through their ties to outsiders who controlled the resources of money and arms.

With the support of foreign aid, the mujahidin were ultimately successful in their jihad to drive out the Soviet forces, but not in their attempts to construct a political alternative to govern Afghanistan after their victory. Throughout the war, the mujahidin were never fully able to replace traditional structures with a modern political system based on Islam. Most mujahidin commanders either used traditional patterns of power, becoming the new *khans*, or sought to adapt modern political structures to the traditional society. In time the prominent leaders accumulated wealth and power and, in contrast to the past, wealth became a determining factor in the delineation of power at all levels.

With the departure of foreign troops and the long sought demise of Kabul's leftist government, The Islamic State of Afghanistan finally came into being in April 1992. This represented a distinct break with Afghan history, for religious specialists had never before exercised state power. But the new government failed to establish its legitimacy and, as much of its financial support dissipated, local and middle range commanders and their militia not only fought among themselves but resorted to a host of unacceptable practices in their protracted scrambles for power and profit. Throughout the nation the populous suffered from harassment, extortion, kidnapping, burglary, hijacking and acts dishonoring women. Drug trafficking increased alarmingly; nowhere were the highways safe. The mujahidin had forfeited the trust they once enjoyed.

In the fall of 1994 a Muslim "student militia" came forth vowing to cleanse the nation of the excesses sullying the jihad. Their avowed intention is to bring in a "pure" Islamic state subject to their own strict interpretations of the Shariah. Many of the leaders of this movement called the Taliban (seekers or students of Islam) were one-time mujahidin themselves, but the bulk of their forces are comprised of young Afghan refugees trained in Pakistani *madrassas* (religious schools), especially those run by the Jamiat-e Ulema-e Islam Pakistan, the aggressively conservative Pakistani political religious party headed by Maulana Fazlur Rahman, arch rival of Qazi Husain Ahmed, leader of the equally conservative Jamaat-e-Islami and long time supporter of the mujahidin.

Headquartered in Kandahar, initially almost entirely Pushtun, predominantly from the rural areas, and from the top leadership down to the fighting militia characteristically in their thirties or forties and even younger, the Taliban swept the country. In

September 1996 they captured Kabul and ruled over two-thirds of Afghanistan.

The meteoric take over went almost unchallenged. Arms were collected and security was established. At the same time, acts committed for the purpose of enforcing the Shariah included public executions for murder, stoning for adultery, amputation for theft, a bann on all forms of gambling such as kite flying, chess and *kawk* (partridge) fighting, prohibition of music and videos, proscriptions against pictures of humans and animals, and an embargo on women's voices over the radio. Women are to remain as invisible as possible, behind the veil, in purdah in their homes, and dismissed from work or study outside their homes. Like many before them, the Taliban wave the flag of women's chasteness to prove their superior Muslimness.

Because of the strong religious sentiments that animate their minds, rural Afghans are still mostly captivated by the Taliban at the beginning of 1997. Others look on appalled at the rigidly orthodox dictates of these self-proclaimed arbiters of Islamic rectitude. To them Taliban interpretations of the Shariah are foreign deviations alien to the Islam practiced in Afghan society which has always stressed moderation, tolerance, dignity, individual choice and egalitarianism.

EDUCATION

Two parallel educational systems function in Afghanistan. Traditional Islamic madrassa found in towns and villages teach children basic moral values and ritual knowledge through the study of the Holy Koran, the *Hadith* (Sayings of the Prophet Mohammad), and popular edited religious texts. Higher level madrassa located in Herat, Kunduz, Ghazni, Kandahar and Kabul were known as important learning centers. Leading religious leaders also attended famous madrassa in India such as the renowned establishment located at Deoband.

The older generation was educated in madrassa or privately at home. The modern educational system was introduced at the end of the nineteenth century by the government which used it as a means to convince traditionalists of the compatibility of Islam with modernization. This system was subsequently expanded with the continued assistance of France, Germany, Turkey, India, Britain, the United States and the Soviet Union.

In 1935, education was declared universal, compulsory and free. With its expansion, the secular system came to be regarded as the principle medium for creating a national ideology and emphasized productive skills while effectively limiting Islamic studies to ritual knowledge. By the 1960s, technical education assumed critical importance because of the surge in development.

Beginning as early as the reign of Amir Abdur Rahman (1880-1901), considerable attention was paid to extending secular elementary schools, lycees and vocational schools to the rural areas. Nevertheless, education remained primarily the prerogative of upper urban groups. By the 1960s as the expanding government apparatus required more bureaucrats, ninety percent of all school graduates were employed by government with the result that the educated tended to be seen by villagers as government officials. Graduates of madrassa sought careers as religious functionaries or judges.

Since 1978, however, a steady decline has all but demolished the educational infrastructure. Afghanistan in 1996 had the highest illiteracy rate in Asia, for both men and women.

Literacy

As with other sectors, statistics are difficult to confirm. Since 1978, particularly, validated nation-wide data have been impossible to obtain with the result that official figures on which much recently published data are based should be employed with great caution.

Nevertheless, pre-war trends when the literacy rate was estimated at 11.4 percent (18.7 percent male; 2.8 female), persist and provide useful patterns reflected in the present. Then, as now, economic, regional and gender bias was very noticeable. Urban-rural and regional disparities are still valid. In urban settings 25.9 percent (35.5 percent male; 14.8 percent female) of the population six years old and over were literate, but in rural areas literate accounted for only 8.8. percent (15.7 percent male; 0.6 percent female, in some provinces 0.1 percent). Regionally, 32 percent of the students attending schools in 1978 lived in the Central region around Kabul, compared with only 3.8 percent living in the East Central mountains of Bamiyan and Ghor. Contrasting 1993 official figures giving an overall literacy rate of 29.8 percent (45.2 percent males; 13.5 percent females) assumes that expanded educational efforts during the intervening years were effective. In reality the bulk of the students represented in the enrollment figures remain functionally illiterate.

Administrative Structure

Although now in shambles, a skeleton education infrastructure based on the past partially remains. Children from age seven attended six years of primary school, three years of middle and three years of secondary school. Most middle and secondary schools were segregated by sex, while primary and higher education were coeducational. The system was, and is, administered centrally through the Ministry of Education which is solely responsible for policy, management and administration, including curriculum and textbooks. Provincial directorates of education are nominally responsible for local administration, but few standard polices apply because of the establishment of a variety of regional authorities since 1992.

Enrollment

A demographic survey conducted in 1976 estimated that 81 percent of the population over six (71 percent male; 93 percent female) had never attended school. Attendance of school-age children declined markedly in the higher grades: primary 30 percent (51 percent male; 8.6 percent female); middle 12 percent (21 percent male; 3.0 percent female); secondary 7 percent (12 percent male; 2 percent female). Although low, this represented more than a two-fold increase from the mid-1960s. Since the war, however, drop-out rates have continued to rise while school completion rates fall, especially among females. By 1990, even official figures record a substantial decline in primary schools: a drop of 84 percent in the number of boys schools; a 72 percent drop for girls. This reflected the physical destruction caused by the war, the refugee exodus, and the scarcity of teachers, a high proportion of whom, male and female, settled in third countries.

Curriculum

Numbers do not tell the full story. The concept that curriculum should be designed so as to enable students to function fully in their own worlds was never understood. For the majority of village children the knowledge they gained at school had scant relevance to their lives and provided little of benefit to compensate for time spent in school. For boys, meaningful learning experiences took place in the fields with their fathers; for girls, at home with mothers, aunts and grandmothers. Rural Afghans for the most part consequently viewed formal education with profound indifference before the war. In addition, since there were are no reading materials to sustain interest, a large percentage of those who dropped out of the system lapsed quickly into illiteracy. Even instruction in reading and writing was weak, causing a disturbing lack of language skills among those pursuing higher studies.

With the advent of invasion and war, many residing in communities outside the control of the Kabul government or in refugees settlements came to view secular education as an alien Western imposition contradicting Islamic values; the road along which communism was brought to Afghanistan; an instrument of Sovietization. This attitude mellowed over the years as many refugees observed the benefits of education, but the curriculadeveloped for refugee children was highly politicized and filled with war messages. Attempts by NGOs to include subjects pertaining to practical life skills, basic health, simple agriculture, environment and cultural awareness were met with indifference by the authorities. The war messages have been discarded but little else has changed. There is still no agreement on curricula despite two years of concerted efforts by the NGOs to arrive at a consensus with local authorities. As a result, several systems are employed.

Teacher Training

Traditional teaching methods seek to ensure memory retention through rote. This method may also be noted in many secular schools in spite of a pre-war network of well-established teacher training institutes in Kabul and major provincial centers which provided 2-year and 4-year courses largely for primary teachers. The Faculty of Education at Kabul University taught pedagogy and administration; other faculties trained teachers in general knowledge and specialized subjects such as literature and languages, geophysics, social science, archaeology, and theology.

Afghan women have always been attracted to the teaching profession because it is regarded as a culturally acceptable career for women. After the war began in 1978, however, many qualified teachers, male and female, opted for resettlement abroad. NGOs seek to fill this gap, but because of limited allocations of funds, salaries are mostly months in arrears, trained male teachers often prefer to work as day laborers while female teachers, even before the Taliban banned women from schools, worked without pay, or stayed at home.

Higher Education

Academic and higher technical education opportunities were well-developed by 1978. The first college of Medicine opened in Kabul in 1932 and later faculties were joined to form Kabul University in 1946; women were admitted in 1960; and all faculties were brought to a central campus in 1964. Kabul University extended its facilities by opening the Nangarhar Faculty of Medicine in Jalalabad in 1963 which formed the nucleus of Ningrahar University in 1964 which has been called the Ningrahar Islamic University since 1992. In addition, over the years increasing numbers of students, male and female, studied abroad.

Support for the university's faculties came from many international sources, including the United States. In 1969 Prime Minister Alexei Kosygin opened the Polytechnic Institute in Kabul where the curriculum included engineering, geology, mineral, oil and gas exploitation, roads and industrial construction, hydroelectric networks and city planning. Later, during the tenure of the PDPA governments, Balkh University (1986), Herat University (1988), and Kandahar University (1991) were established. In the mid-1990s, institutions were opened in Baghlan, Takhar and Bamiyan. Most higher education institutions were still functioning in 1996, albeit in severely damaged physical facilities, with next to no textbooks, libraries or laboratories, and hampered by underqualified staff. The Taliban exclude women from universities in areas under their control.

Adult Literacy

Functional literacy courses which had existed since the 1950s were considerably developed during the 1970s, along with appropriate teaching and reading materials for new literate. The politicized promotion of adult literacy by the PDPA after 1978, however, was greatly resented. In the 1990s, aid providers enthusiastically sponsor adult courses, but it is difficult for new literate to maintain their acquired skills because insufficient attention is given to producing suitable reading materials.

Current Activities

Teacher training, textbook development, supplementary readings, curricula, school supplies and construction are all emphasized by agencies assisting Afghanistan's education sector. In many instances, literacy and numeracy are combined with, health, dental care, demining, agriculture and other skills training. Goals emphasize literacy for productivity so as to build human capacities, but, as in the past, social needs are secondary. According to the 1995 work plan prepared by twenty-six Afghan and international NGOs and three UN agencies, their programs serve 20 provinces. Again, provinces such as Ghor, Bamiyan, Nimroz and Badakhshan continue to be neglected.

Despite these efforts, education receives only about 10 percent of the funding provided for other sectors. Schools are still withoutbuildings in many areas and sustainability is questionable because of insufficient coordination, underutilized trained teachers, inattention to quality improvement, inadequate teaching materials, monitoring, and evaluation.

Not enough attention has been made to devise special education courses to reach young, one-time mujahideen who opted to go to war instead of completing their education. These restive individuals are unable to submit to constructive discipline such as school attendance, yet they have no technical competence to enable them to contribute productively to the society. Existing programs, therefore, fall far short in human resource capacity building which is arguably the most crucial need facing Afghanistan today.

In areas administered by the Taliban, emphasis is placed on maximizing religious subjects, schools for girls are closed and female teachers are forbidden to teach. Many NGOs, on instruction from their donors, have suspended assistance in those areas where female education is curtailed. Others seek alternative options such as home schools, but the education system as a whole is beset with grave limitations on key issues such as equitable access and quality instruction. Several future generations will be severely handicapped as a result.

[RESERVED]

HEALTH

Before the war, the health situation in Afghanistan was among the worst in the world primarily because the health infrastructure was grossly inadequate and mostly limited to urban centers. Protracted conflict since 1978 worsened the inequitable distribution of health manpower and services. The estimated infant mortality rate was 163 per 1000 live births (1993); the under five mortality rate 257 for every 1000 live births (1994); the maternal mortality rate 1700 per 100,000 live births (1993); and life expectancy at birth was 43.7.

Since infant and under five mortality rates are frequently used as reliable overall indicators of community health and development, these figures underscore the appalling state of the health sector in Afghanistan. Most children die of a variety of infectious and parasitic diseases, including acute diarrhoea, respiratory infections, tuberculosis, diphtheria, poliomyelitis, malaria, measles and malnutrition, in addition to disorders allied to pregnancy and delivery.

The tragedy is that 80 to 85 percent of these diseases can be avoided by preventive measures and by the provision of proper health care, or cured at an affordable cost. However, currently there is only one health center to care for every population group of approximately 100,000. Only 12 percent of pregnant women have access to maternal and emergency obstetric care; only 38 percent of children under one year are fully immunized. These problems are compounded by the fact that fully three-quarters of the nations physicians have left the country resulting in a physician/patient ratio of over 95,000/1. Because of the inadequacy of the health delivery system, a majority of the population relies on indigenous healers such as traditional midwives, herbalists, bone setters and barbers who circumcise, let blood, pull teeth, and perform other curative procedures. Mullahs, sayyids and other specialists prepare curative and protective amulets.

The war and deteriorating economic, social, and physical conditions in both rural and most urban areas, have impaired housing and environmental sanitation facilities in general and added sinister dimensions. By the end of 1996, it was estimated that 1.5 million men women and children were physically disabled by war injuries, including amputation, blindness and paralysis, as well as debilitating infectious diseases, such as poliomyelitis and leprosy. Birth complications causing disabilities such as cerebral palsy and mental retardation also increased. Another 10 percent of the total population representing families and associates of the disabled are directly affected by these disabilities. They require information and instruction not only regarding physical care, but also in ways to integrate disabled persons into communities as respected and productive members.

Sadly, the number of disabled increases daily because of an estimated 10 million landmines and unexploded ordnance (UXO) that contaminate the landscape, the largest concentration in the world. A 1993 national survey revealed there were over 465 square kilometers of minefield, of which 113 square kilometers were high priority areas directly affecting residential areas, farm lands, grazing pastures and canals; subsequently further high priority areas totalling more than ninety square kilometers were identified; and, as refugees return, new minefields continue to be uncovered raising low priority areas to high priority. By the end of 1996 some 158.8 square kilometers were cleared and 300,000 mines destroyed. The UN Mine Clearance Programme in cooperation with eight NGOs, includes 50 demining teams and 10 mine dog groups, as well as male and female mine awareness teams, staffed by some 3,000 Afghans. Due to continuing hostilities, however, several de-mined areas have been re-mined. It will be many years before Afghanistan will be free of this menace.

Assistance to enhance the capacity and increase the accessibility of health services, emphasizes basic preventive and curative primary health services, with special attention to strengthening Mother Child Health and health man power development at all levels, including Traditional Birth Attendants and community

180

health workers. Providing safe potable water sources and sanitation facilities is also a high priority since contaminated water sources are major causes of high morbidity and mortality. Upwards of 60 NGOs, in addition to the International Red Cross Committee and the International Federation of Red Cross and Red Crescent Societies, WHO and UNICEF have been active in the health sector over the years, assisting everything from regional, provincial and district hospitals to basic health clinics, as well as specialized services in physiotherapy, drug detoxification, TB and malaria control.

The Mass Immunization Campaigns launched by WHO and UNICEF, in partnership with the Ministry of Public Health, utilizing a cadre of more than 15,000 vaccinators, health workers and volunteers throughout the country, are singular successes accomplished with the active cooperation of all parties to the conflict. In 1995, 2.6 million were vaccinated against DPT and measles; in 1996 2.3 million children under five received oral polio vaccine; during 1997, the nation-wide goal is to reach approximately four million children under five, in addition to 60 percent of women of child bearing age. The ultimate aim is to totally eradicate the polio virus in Afghanistan.

As in the case with the education sector, however, the overall results are generally spotty. New and refurbished buildings intended to dispense medical care stand empty because of lack of personnel or equipment; some have been commandeered by political groups for offices. Of the thousands trained in various medical fields, few find employment. Databases list increasing numbers of "discontinued" projects and facilities. This is particularly disheartening because the lack of medical facilities is a major deterrent to refugee repatriation.

REFUGEES AND REPATRIATION

Eighteen years after the 1978 coup by the PDPA, the refugee problem remained a significant issue for Afghanistan and its neighbors. The refugee flow began as a trickle in April 1978, reaching a peak during the first half of 1981 when an estimated 4,700 crossed the Pakistan border daily. The flow ebbed and surged in response to Soviet offenses, so that by the fall of 1989, the number of Afghan refugees was estimated at 3.2 million in Pakistan, 2.2. million in Iran, and several hundred thousands resettled in scattered communities throughout the world. Afghans represented the largest single concentration of refugees in the world on whom an estimated $1 million a day was expended in 1988.

Following the fall of the PDPA regime in 1992, a new wave of refugees entered Pakistan; the takeover of Kabul by the Taliban in 1996 set in motion a lesser flow which continued in 1997 although refugee assistance, other than to those most vulnerable, was cut back drastically in October 1995. Only emergency assistance is available in hastily reconstituted camps for new arrivals around Peshawar.

Unlike earlier flows of refugees who fled from the consequences of war, recent arrivals are largely educated urban families fleeing because the economy has broken down and, most significantly, because education for girls is unavailable and that provided for boys is so poor. Arriving in Pakistan with high hopes, the new refugees find the situation as bad, if not worse than it is in Afghanistan. There are no jobs, housing and services are expensive as is admission to Pakistani schools, and the schools run by many Afghans are mostly shams. Immigration to third countries is all but closed. Most families, therefore, must depend exclusively on relatives which is psychologically destructive.

Less publicized, but equally disruptive, was the displacement of internal populations, from war affected rural areas to cities, and from bombed out cities to rural areas. IDPs or Internally Displaced Persons are estimated at about one million. UNHCR, ICRC and NGO-assisted camps were established in and around Jalalabad in the east, at Pul-i-Khumri, Mazar-i- Sharif and Kunduz in the north, and in Herat in the west. Other IDPs survived on the goodwill and support systems of loc ' rural communities. This stretched the resources of towns and rural areas throughout the country, especially south and north of Kabul and in the Hazarajat. These movements could bring about changes in demographic balances with untold consequences.

To stem the flow of refugees, NGOs based in Pakistan led by the example of the Swedish Committee for Afghanistan in 1982, provided essential services in health, education and agriculture inside Afghanistan. These were known as cross-border programs. At the same time, UN agencies, delivered cross-line assistance into mujahideen-held from their offices in Kabul.

In July 1990 UNHCR started an assisted repatriation program in Pakistan, later extended to Iran. By the end of 1996 total repatriation reached 3.84 million. Many returnees were assisted by Quick Impact Projects. Designed to encourage repatriation and facilitate refugees when they returned, the QIP provided assistance for a limited period to support improvements in shelter, health and sanitation, and education, repaired roads and irrigation systems, and offered skills training related to income generation. Many Afghan NGOs also seek to support the sustainable return of refugees and IDPs by strengthening livelihood security, improving economic opportunities, providing basic social safety nets and restoring the environment.

Following Taliban takeovers of Jalalabad and Kabul in September 1996, the flow of returnees decreased dramatically - on some days none crossed the border - while the number of families crossing into Pakistan once again rose, despite the fact that they were officially discouraged from entering and that only minimum emergency assistance was available.

The background and origins of the refugees has changed over

the years. The first to come in 1978 were members of the extended Afghan royal family, their associates, and political allies. Almost all resettled in third countries. By the mid-1980s, most refugees in Pakistan were rural, nonliterate pastoralists and farmers. The refugees who fled from Kabul in the 1990s included educated urban bureaucrats, uneducated laborers and high profile officials. Most of the latter were immediately given asylum in third countries. By 1996 the majority of arrivals were highly urbanized, skilled professionals and technocrats. In Pakistan they sit idle, representing a tragic waste of scarce human resources at the very moment in the nation's history when their skills are so desperately needed for reconstruction.

In the early years most refugees, with the exception of those from urban areas who chose to live in cities, lived in tented villages in the North West Frontier Province (NWFP), in Baluchistan Province, and in southwest Punjab. Over the years many of these villages became permanent settlements, with mud-brick dwellings and walled compounds replicating the rural villages inside Afghanistan. Pakistan government policies concerning refugees has all along been most liberal. No barbed-wire fences confine camps, and refugees are free to move anywhere to seek employment. Additionally, management of supplies and services provided by the Pakistan government, UNHCR and numbers of NGOs was exemplary. Remarkably, there were no epidemics, little malnutrition because of delayed or insufficient food, and no major outbreaks of violence between refugee and local populations.

Social life for most refugees in Pakistan retained many elements of life in Afghanistan, although settlement patterns in an alien environment with indiscriminate mixings of family, geographic, ethnic, sectarian and social groups strengthened inherent social and religious conservatism. Family bonds were strengthened, but the outward semblance of solidity masked an existence that was tenuous and subject to severe tensions, many of which marginalized traditional female roles and curtailed their freedom. Aggressive campaigns by mujahideen parties whose representatives largely controlled the refugee camps kept women from seeking employment and training opportunities. Many of these problems gradually disappeared in 1992 once the mujahideen took over the reins of government in Kabul.

On the other hand, although still physically restricted, women have widened their horizons and heightened their expectations, especially with regard to better health and education. Many women are thus reluctant to repatriate, citing an unwillingness once again to undergo the traumas of displacement, the inability of the authorities to provide even minimal services to which they have become accustomed, and the absence of guaranteed economic security. A million or more refugees remain in Pakistan, therefore, and the prospects for total repatriation are less than bright.

[RESERVED]

WARFARE AND CIVIC CULTURE

The Soviet-Afghan war has caused grave injury to the civic culture of Afghanistan. The destruction and disruption wrought by the magnitude of the lethal technology employed was exponentially greater than that of any previous invasion in the past. In addition to extensive ecological damage, including the vicious destruction of Kabul that dwarfs anything previously experienced, the war stretched taught the fabric of the society, threatening to undermine its confidence.

National traits once honored hallmarks of Afghan character were jeopardized. Tolerance for others. Forthrightness. Aversion to fanatics. Respect for women. Loyalty to colleagues and classmates. Dislike for ostentation. Commitment to academic freedom. All were compromised.

Two generations of children have grown up without knowing the joys of childhood, their lives concentrated instead on how to avoid death and deal with emotions associated with death. The war has left terrible scars on minds as well as bodies. These scars threaten to undermine the traditional social infrastructure which served for decades to dampen ethnic, religious, cultural and linguistic differences in this complex multicultural society.

The deep apprehensions, amounting to fear among many, that prevail under Taliban rule despite an acknowledged improvement in security, have resulted in the breakdown of trust which makes the organization of cooperative community projects difficult. This compounds the fact that many Afghans who benefitted from largely free services while in exile developed complacent attitudes leading them to expect others to do for them what once they expected to do for themselves. Their vaunted self-reliance was thus eroded.

The spirit of jihad that initially sustained the leaders as a vital animating force deteriorated as spirals of continuing conflict and individual struggles for self-aggrandizement created a previously unknown lust for money in the pursuit of which hallowed values were violated without precedent. The very soul of Afghanistan's cultural heritage was assaulted by the systematic looting of the Kabul Museum and pillaging of archaeological sites throughout the country. These were not spontaneous acts committed by victorious armies, but calculated thefts for profit without regard to national pride or the preservation of its cultural identity.

Fueled by this voracious appetite for illicit gains, the production of opium in Afghanistan tripled during 1979-89, and then again quadrupled from 1989-96 accounting for 40 percent of the world's opium production. Afghanistan stands now just below Burma on the international narcotics scene, accounting for about 30 percent of global production. The largest areas under poppy cultivation are in the provinces of Hilmand and Nangrahar where 80 percent of Afghanistan's opium poppies are grown in fields formerly producing food and cash crops. The absence of law enforcement facilities makes these one of the least controlled narcotics trafficking areas in the world.

Happily, although many believe that the number of Afghan heroin addicts has increased, no reliable data indicate that the abuse of hard drugs is yet a significant problem. Nevertheless, those Afghans who are partners in this industry are eager to subvert any individual or institution that would restrict their operations.

The Taliban seek to redress this situation but the breakdown of governance hampers their efforts. Senior authorities are untrained and thus incapable of formulating consistent policies or strategies for reconstruction; even when policies are announced, the intent to carry them out is not always clear. As a result, the bureaucracy is overcome with inertia, except for the imposition of external forms of selective Islamic conduct, such as beards for men and veils for women.

To revitalize this otherwise turgid bureaucracy will require monumental efforts. Institution-building with concomitant human resource development are urgent priorities. Almost two generations of young Afghan men opted for war instead of education; educational opportunities for women were severely curtailed for many years and are now all but nonexistent; the education system is in shambles. Thus those who should be most productive today are emotionally and mentally unprepared and highly vulnerable to the temptations of anti-social activities.

The collapse of the old order of governance highlights the artificiality of the systems conceived by rulers in building a framework of unity in the name of a nation-state on the unstable foundation of Afghanistan's multifaceted society. Whether the systems were expressed in terms of constitutional or Islamic principles, the controversies and contentions between the state, the religious establishment and local leadership arrangements have never been satisfactorily addressed.

While acknowledging the truth of social aberrations and political intransigence, it must also be noted that Afghan society continues to exhibit a dynamic meld of change and continuity. Old values have by no means been discarded by the bulk of the society who still hold fast to the standards detailed throughout this chapter. The concepts of honor and hospitality, combined with the essence of Islam's teachings embodying honesty, generosity, frugality, fairness, tolerance and respect for others still underlies the every day life of most Afghans. A spirit of courageous conviction that viable solutions will ultimately evolve is abundantly evident as the Afghans face their uncertain future with quiet dignity. This characteristic of Afghan society remains inviolate.

The current challenge before the Afghans is indeed daunting. But, so too were the challenges presented after 1978 by coups, invasion and occupation. Although many may now call for the UN to find solutions, others are equally convinced that as Afghans they cannot wait for others, that peace cannot be brought by outsiders. For them, solutions lie in the patient rebuilding of confidence and trust within individual communities.

Recent events have brought about sweeping changes. There can be no return to what was pre-war Afghanistan. Nevertheless, the society that will emerge will be rooted in the past. Despite the virulence of the recent onslaughts, despite current deplorable erosions and perversions, continuity will in the end permit shared sets of values to prevail along with the variations and varieties that constitute the richness of Afghanistan's cultural heritage. Afghan culture has been constantly changing; adaptability is a measure of its strength.

* * *

Louis Dupree's *Afghanistan* remains the most comprehensive discussion on cultural patterns, from the prehistoric through 1980. Among the many analytical studies of the *jihad* period since 1978, Asta Olesen in *Islam and Politics in Afghanistan* provides a clear picture of tribal ideologies and their relationships with ruling authorities since Ahmad Shah Durrani in the eighteenth century. For the Russian perspective on the conflict after 1978, Gennady Bocharov's reflective *Russian Roulette: Afghanistan Through Russian Eyes* recreates the atmosphere and moral enigmas of war.

In a novel approach using stories told about the lives of three prominent historical figures in the late nineteenth century, David Edwardes in *Heroes of the Age* sheds new light on the contemporary strife by examining values in Pushtun culture, especially as they contend with state encroachments during the imposition of the concept of nation-state on such a diverse culture. The fourteen contributors to *Fundamentalism Reborn?: Afghanistan Under the Taliban* edited by William Maley, address the origins of the Taliban Movement as well as the cultural dilemmas inherent in this most recent attempt to fuse society's diverse segments into a confined mold.

An overview of the cultural traumas experienced by Afghan refugees, especially women, may be found in *Disposable People? The Plight of Refugees* by Judy Mayotte, while the complexities and challenges involved in reconstruction is provocatively described by Asger Christensen in *Aiding Afghanistan: The Background and Prospects for Reconstruction in a Fragmented Society.*

Of the many specific ethnographic studies listed in the bibliography, those by Barfield, Boesen, Canfield, Christensesn, Dor, L. Dupree, Ferdinand, Frederiksen, Glatzer, Harpviken, Olesen, Pedersen, Rao, Shahrani, N. Tapper and R. Tapper are particularly recommended, as is the comprehensive study on the variety of house-types illustrated in *Afghanistan: An Atlas of Indigenous Domestic Architecture* by Albert Szabo and Thomas Barfield.

People cannot be understood in isolation from the landscape which shapes their lives. The stunning vividness of Afghanistan's environment captured in the work of Roland and Sabrina Michaud is published in *Afghanistan* and *Mirror of the Orient.*

Data as of 1997

Index

Abdul Rashid . . . . XXI, XXII, 110, 215

ABDUR RAHMAN KHAN . . . . XLV, 2, 31, 104

Achaemenid . . . . XLV, 5

Achaemenid Rule . . . . XLV, 5

Administrative Structure . . . . XLVII, 171

Adult Literacy . . . . XLVII, 174

Afghan Persian (Dari) 212

age 17, 20, 131, 147, 171, 181, 192, 210, 212, 214, 225

agriculture . . . XIII, XIV, XXV, 94, 109, 125, 128, 129, 172, 175,
184, 218, 220

AHMAD SHAH . . . XVI, XLV, 2, 17-21, 66, 73, 75, 78, 105, 107,
115, 122, 163, 192, 215

AHMAD SHAH AND THE DURRANI EMPIRE . XLV, 17, 105

Ahmad Shah Masood 107, 215

Aimaq . . . . XIII, XV, XLVI, 111, 126

airports 224

Alexander . . . . XV, XLV, 5, 6, 24, 113

Alexander 5, 6, 24, 113

Alexander and Greek Rule . . . . XLV, 6

Arab . . . . . XVI, XXX, XLIII, XLVI, 11, 111, 112, 126, 149, 154

Asian 7, 8, 11, 37, 89, 90, 94

Badakhshan 93, 106-109, 111, 112, 156, 175, 213

Badghis 91, 93, 108, 111, 213

Baghlan 93, 106, 111, 156, 157, 174, 213

Balkh . . . . XVI, 5, 8, 93, 110, 150, 154, 174, 213

Balochi 212

Baluch . . . . XIII, XV, XXX, XLVI, 111, 114, 118, 126, 127

195

Bamian 8, 26, 27, 213

barites . . . . XIV, XXVII, 209

birth rate 100, 210

Brahui . . . . XLVI, 114

Central Asian and Sassanian Rule . . . . XLV, 7

chromite . . . . XIV, XXVII, 209

climate . . . . XIII, XLVI, 14, 61, 89, 94, 96, 208, 209

coal . . . . XIV, XXVII, 209, 219

coastline 208

COMMUNISM . . . . XLVI, 73, 77, 172

Consolidation of the Modern State . . . . XLV, 31

copper . . . . XIV, XXVII, 209, 219

Current Activities . . . . XLVII, 175

Curriculum . . . . XLVII, 171, 172, 174

Daoud . . . . XVIV, XIX, XLV, 55, 60-64, 66, 69-73

Daoud as Prime Minister . . . . XLIV, 60

DAOUD'S REPUBLIC . . . . XVIV, XLV, 69

death rate 100, 210

Dost Mohammad . . . . XLV, 21, 23-26, 28, 37, 47, 52, 122

DURRANI . XVI, XLV, 2, 17, 20, 21, 66, 104-107, 115, 119, 122,
123, 126, 163, 192

DURRANI EMPIRE . . . . XLV, 17, 105

Early Development of Islam . . . . XLVII, 147

Early Links with the Soviet Union . . . . XLV, 58

earthquakes 94, 209

EDUCATION . . XIII, XXIII, XXVIII, XLVII, 44, 116, 131, 134,
138, 141, 142, 144, 145, 155, 159, 160, 169, 171-
175, 181, 183, 184, 186, 191

elevation 208

emirate . . . . XIII, XXIV, 213

Enrollment . . . . XLVII, 170, 171

Ethnic Groups . . XIII, XLVI, 11, 18, 19, 104, 116, 118-120, 122, 128, 131, 135, 137, 157, 160, 165, 212

exchange rates 221

Experiment with Liberalized Politics . . . . XLV, 59

exports . . . . XIV, XXVII, 219, 220

FAMILY . XVII-XIX, XXXVI, XLVI, 32, 44, 45, 51, 52, 55, 60, 63, 64, 72, 73, 86, 103, 105, 106, 114, 116, 117, 122, 129, 131-138, 141-145, 147, 153, 154, 157-161, 185

Farah 93, 158, 213

Farsiwan . . . . XLVI, 113, 155

Faryab 93, 109, 111, 114, 158, 213

Flag . . . . XIV, 167, 216

flooding 95, 96, 209

forests 92, 209

GENDER ROLES . . . . XLVII, 141, 143

Geography . . . . XIII, 86, 93, 207, 210

Ghaznavid . . . . XLV, 12

Ghaznavid and Ghorid Rule . . . . XLV, 12

Ghazni . . . XVI, XXVIII, 12, 17, 26, 93, 100, 113, 117, 150, 154, 155, 169, 213, 222

Ghorid . . . . XLV, 12

Ghowr 213

government . . . V, XIV, XIX, XX, XXII-XXVI, XXVIII, XXIX, XXXIII-XXXVI, XXXIX, 23, 25, 26, 31, 32, 37, 42-44, 55-66, 70, 73, 74, 76, 78, 99, 100, 106, 107, 111, 113, 118, 119, 131, 134, 141, 144, 158, 160, 161,

164-166, 169, 172, 185, 186, 212-214, 222

Greek .... XLV, 6, 47

harbors 224

Hazara .... XIII, XV, XXIII, XLVI, 18, 108, 109, 111, 115, 118, 119, 155, 212

HEALTH .... XIII, XXXV, XXXVI, XLVII, 144, 172, 175, 179-181, 184, 186

heliports 225

Helmand .... XXXI, 37, 56, 58, 60, 213

Herat ... XIII, XVI, XX, XXVIII, XXXI, 6, 12-14, 17, 20, 24, 25, 28, 91, 93, 104, 109-111, 113, 150, 154, 155, 157, 158, 165, 169, 174, 184, 213, 222

Higher Education .... XLVII, 171, 173, 174

highways .... XXVIII, 166, 223

HIV/AIDS 211, 212

industries 63, 129, 219

infant mortality .... XIII, 100, 179, 211

Interethnic Relations .... XLVI, 118

Iran ... XIII, XIV, XXVI-XXVIII, XXXI, XLII, 2, 3, 5, 7, 11, 12, 14, 15, 17, 20, 24, 37, 55, 56, 61, 71-74, 76, 78, 89, 93, 95, 99, 114, 127, 149, 150, 183, 184, 207, 208, 210, 217, 220, 222

iron ore .... XXVII, 209

ISLAMIC ... XIII-XV, XXI-XXIV, XXX, XXXI, XXXIII, XLV, XLVII, 2, 5, 11-13, 18, 45, 55, 72, 77, 85, 90, 105, 107, 116, 136-138, 144, 148-152, 154-156, 158-160, 163, 164, 166, 167, 169, 172, 173, 190, 191, 207, 213-216, 226

ISLAMIC CONQUEST .... XLV, 11

ISLAMIC CONQUEST 11

Islamic Expression in Afghanistan .... XLVII, 154

Ismailis .... XLVII, 155-157

Ithna Ashariya (Twelver or Imami) Shia .... XLVII, 155

Jat .... XLVI, 117

Jowzjan 213

Kabol 213

Kabul ...... XIII, XVI-XVIII, XX, XXII-XXIV, XXVIII, XXX,
XXXIV, XXXV, 7, 13-15, 17, 19, 20, 23-29, 34, 38,
41-45, 47, 48, 58-61, 66, 70, 73-76, 78, 90-93, 95,
100, 105-107, 109, 116, 117, 141, 155-158, 164,
165, 167, 169, 170, 172-174, 183-186, 189, 190,
213, 214, 216, 221, 222

Kabuli .... XLVI, 116, 157

Kandahar . XIII, XX, XXIII, XXVIII, 92, 93, 105, 113, 116, 154,
155, 158, 166, 169, 174, 213, 222

Kapisa 93, 213

Khowst 213

KING AMANULLAH .... XVII, XLV, 41, 123, 141, 163

KING HABIBULLAH .... XLV, 37

Kirghiz .... XLVI, 24, 33, 112, 126, 128

Konar 213

Kondoz 213

labor .... XXV, 44, 126, 127, 144, 217, 218

Laghman 93, 113, 117, 213

land .... XIX, XX, XXV, XXIX, 11, 31, 74, 85, 89, 92, 106, 108,
118, 127-129, 207-209, 221

lead .... XIV, XXVII, XXX, 74, 91, 121, 152, 153, 160, 209

life expectancy .... XIII, 100, 179, 211

Literacy .... XIII, XLVII, 170, 174, 175, 212

Lowgar 213

Meaning and Practice . . . . XLVII, 159

military . . XVIII, XX, XXIV, XXXI, XXXII, XXXIV, 12, 19, 27-29, 33, 41, 43, 61, 62, 66, 69, 71-73, 75, 77, 91, 107, 119, 141, 165, 215, 217, 225, 226

Mixed Subsistence Patterns . . . . XLVI, 128

Modernization and Development of Institutions . . . . XLV, 32

MOHAMMAD ZAHIR SHAH . . . . XVIII, XLV, 55

Mongol . . . . XVI, XLV, 2, 13, 19, 108

Mongol Rule . . . . XLV, 13

Mountains . . . XIII, XLVI, 19, 89, 90, 92-95, 106, 107, 112, 126, 129, 170, 208, 209

Mughal . . . . XLV, 13-15, 17, 18

Mughal-Safavid Rivalry XLV

MUHAMMAD NADIR SHAH . . . . XLV, 51

Nangarhar 93, 173, 213

natural gas . . . . XIV, XXVII, 209, 219, 224

Nimruz 213

Non-Muslims XLVI

nuclear 77, 126, 132, 137, 209, 219

Nurestan (Nuristan) 213

Nuristani . . . . XIII, XLVI, 113, 119, 120, 144

Oruzgan 213

Pakistan . . XIII, XIV, XVIII, XXI, XXIII, XXVI-XXVIII, XXX, XXXI, XXXIV, XXXV, XLIII, 11, 12, 33, 56-58, 60-63, 71-75, 77-79, 89, 91-95, 99, 104, 112-114, 116, 127, 128, 131, 132, 138, 149, 157, 166, 183-186, 207, 208, 215, 217, 220

Paktia 213

Paktika 213

Parvan 213

Pashai 212

Pashtu 19, 104, 212

Pashtun . XIII, XVI, XVIII, XXIII, XXX, XLVI, 5, 11, 14, 15, 17-
20, 23, 31, 33, 41-43, 45, 47, 56-58, 60-66, 69, 71,
72, 104, 120, 212, 214, 215

Pastoralism . . . . XLVI, 125, 128

petroleum . . . . XIV, XXVII, 58, 209, 220, 224

pipelines 224

Politicized Islam . . . . XLVII, 163, 164

population   XIII, XV, XVI, XXVI, XLVI, 57, 66, 78, 86, 99, 100,
104, 108, 110, 111, 113, 116, 125, 127, 137, 144,
170, 171, 179, 180, 210-212, 217, 218

ports 224

Qizilbash . . . . XLVI, 20, 23, 104, 115, 118, 155

Rabbani . . . . XIV, XXII, XXIII, XXV, 75, 107, 214, 215

radio 62, 167, 222

railways . . . . XXVIII, 223

REBELLION . XVII, XLVI, 19, 26, 28, 45, 47, 51, 69, 73, 74, 80,
148

Reform, Popular Reaction, and Forced Abdication . . . . . XLV, 43

REFUGEES . . XIII, XXI, XXII, XXIX, XXXIII, XXXV, XLVII,
76, 77, 79, 99, 100, 116, 128, 131, 138, 166, 172,
180, 183-186, 192, 210, 215, 217, 221

REFUGEES AND REPATRIATION . . . . XLVII, 183

Regions . . . XXXVI, XXXIX, XLVI, 5, 6, 14, 32, 33, 91-95, 112,
120, 126, 165

RELIGION . . . . XLVII, 5, 7, 64, 143, 147, 149, 151, 164

Rivers . . . . XLVI, 92, 95

Safavid . . . . XLV, 13, 15, 115 salt .... XIV, XXVII, 209

Samangan 93, 106, 213

Sar-e Pol 213

Sassanian .... XLV, 7, 8, 11

Saudi Arabia .... XXI, XXX, XLIII, 71, 72, 77, 78, 149, 207

sex 171, 211

Shia . XLVII, 11, 76, 105, 106, 108, 109, 115, 148-152, 154-159,
161, 162

SOCIAL STRUCTURE .... XLVI, 103, 109

SOVIET INTERVENTION 73

Soviet Union .... XVIII-XXI, XXVI-XXIX, XXXII, XL, XLIII,
XLV, 6, 11, 42, 55, 56, 58, 60-62, 69-71, 73, 77-79,
86, 93, 127, 138, 147, 169, 207

stones .... XIV, XXVII, 2, 162, 209

Sufis .... XLVII, 149, 150, 157, 159

Sufism .... XLVII, 149, 150, 155, 157, 159

sulfur .... XIV, XXVII, 209

Sunni . XIII, XV, XLVII, 3, 11, 12, 105, 106, 108-115, 119, 148-
152, 154-157, 161, 212

Sunni and Shia Islam .... XLVII, 148

Sunnis of the Hanafi School .... XLVII, 155

Tajik .... XIII, XV, XVIII, XXIII, XXV, XXXII, XXXIII, XLV,
XLVI, 18, 45, 47, 51, 75, 105-107, 109, 112, 115,
119, 156, 212

TAJIK RULE .... XLV, 47

Takhar 93, 106, 111, 174, 213

talc .... XIV, XXVII, 209

Taliban . XIII-XV, XXIII-XXVII, XXX-XXXII, XXXIV, XXXV,
105, 110, 116, 128, 138, 142, 166, 167, 173-175,
183, 184, 189, 190, 192, 207, 213-216

Teacher Training .... XLVII, 173, 175

telephone .... XXXV, 222

television 222

Tenets of Islam .... XLVII, 151

terrain .... XIII, XXVII, 89, 126, 129, 208

The First Anglo-Afghan War XLV

THE GREAT GAME .... XVII, XLV, 23, 24

The King Reigns: The Last Decade of the Monarchy ... XLV, 63

THE NATURAL ENVIRONMENT .... XLVI, 89

The Pashtunistan Issue .... XLV, 57, 58, 60-62, 69, 71

THE PRE-ISLAMIC PERIOD XLV

THE REIGN OF KING AMANULLAH .... XLV, 41

The Rise of Dost Mohammad .... XLV, 23

The Second Anglo-Afghan War XLV

THE SOCIETY AND ITS ENVIRONMENT XLVI

Third Anglo-Afghan War and Independence XLV

total fertility 211

Tribes ... XXX, XLV, 7, 11, 14, 15, 17-20, 26, 27, 31-33, 42, 43,
                45, 47, 57, 104, 105, 110, 121, 122, 165

Turkic .... XVI, 11, 108-112, 212

Turkmen ...... XIII, XV, XLVI, 18, 24, 104, 110, 111, 126, 212

UNIFSA 215

Uzbek .. XIII, XV, XXI, XXII, XLVI, 18, 51, 109-111, 119, 120,
                126, 212

Vardak 213

Wakhi .... XLVI, 112, 156

WARFARE .... XLVII, 8, 78, 189

WARFARE AND CIVIC CULTURE .... XLVII, 189

waterways 223

Zabol 213

Zahir Shah .... XVIII, XLV, 55, 63, 66, 76

zinc .... XIV, XXVII, 209

Extract on Afghanistan: World Factbook 2001

Afghanistan   **Introduction**

Background: Afghanistan was invaded and occupied by the Soviet Union in 1979. The USSR was forced to withdraw 10 years later by anti-communist mujahidin forces supplied and trained by the US, Saudi Arabia, Pakistan, and others. Fighting subsequently continued among the various mujahidin factions, but the fundamentalist Islamic Taliban movement has been able to seize most of the country. In addition to the continuing civil strife, the country suffers from enormous poverty, a crumbling infrastructure, and widespread land mines.

Afghanistan   **Geography**

Location: Southern Asia, north and west of Pakistan, east of Iran

Geographic coordinates: 33 00 N, 65 00 E

Map references: Asia

Area: *total:* 647,500 sq km

land: 647,500 sq km

water: 0 sq km

**Area -
comparative:** slightly smaller than Texas

**Land
boundaries:** *total:* 5,529 km

border countries: China 76 km, Iran 936 km, Pakistan 2,430 km, Tajikistan 1,206 km, Turkmenistan 744 km, Uzbekistan 137 km

Coastline: 0 km (landlocked)

**Maritime
claims:** none (landlocked)

Climate: arid to semiarid; cold winters and hot summers

Terrain: mostly rugged mountains; plains in north and southwest

**Elevation
extremes:** *lowest point:* Amu Darya 258 m

highest point: Nowshak 7,485 m

Natural resources: natural gas, petroleum, coal, copper, chromite, talc, barites, sulfur, lead, zinc, iron ore, salt, precious and semiprecious stones

Land use: *arable land:* 12%

permanent crops: 0%

permanent pastures: 46%

forests and woodland: 3%

other: 39% (1993 est.)

Irrigated land: 30,000 sq km (1993 est.)

Natural hazards: damaging earthquakes occur in Hindu Kush mountains; flooding; droughts

Environment - current issues: soil degradation; overgrazing; deforestation (much of the remaining forests are being cut down for fuel and building materials); desertification

Environment - international agreements: *party to:* Desertification, Endangered Species, Environmental Modification, Marine Dumping, Nuclear Test Ban

signed, but not ratified: Biodiversity, Climate Change, Hazardous Wastes, Law of the Sea, Marine Life Conservation

**Geography -
note:** landlocked

Afghanistan   **People**

Population: 26,813,057 (July 2001 est.)

Age structure: *0-14 years:* 42.2% (male 5,775,921; female 5,538,836)

15-64 years: 55.01% (male 7,644,242; female 7,106,568)

65 years and over: 2.79% (male 394,444; female 353,046) (2001 est.)

Population growth rate: 3.48% (2001 est.)

note: this rate reflects the continued return of refugees from Iran

Birth rate: 41.42 births/1,000 population (2001 est.)

Death rate: 17.72 deaths/1,000 population (2001 est.)

Net migration rate: 11.11 migrant(s)/1,000 population (2001 est.)

Sex ratio: *at birth:* 1.05 male(s)/female

under 15 years: 1.04 male(s)/female

15-64 years: 1.08 male(s)/female

65 years and over: 1.12 male(s)/female

total population: 1.06 male(s)/female (2001 est.)

Infant mortality rate: 147.02 deaths/1,000 live births (2001 est.)

Life expectancy at birth: *total population:* 46.24 years

male: 46.97 years

female: 45.47 years (2001 est.)

Total fertility rate: 5.79 children born/woman (2001 est.)

HIV/AIDS - adult prevalence rate: less than 0.01% (1999 est.)

HIV/AIDS - people living with HIV/AIDS: NA

HIV/AIDS - NA
deaths:

Nationality: *noun:* Afghan(s)

adjective: Afghan

Ethnic groups: Pashtun 38%, Tajik 25%, Hazara 19%, minor ethnic groups (Aimaks, Turkmen, Baloch, and others) 12%, Uzbek 6%

Religions: Sunni Muslim 84%, Shi'a Muslim 15%, other 1%

Languages: Pashtu 35%, Afghan Persian (Dari) 50%, Turkic languages (primarily Uzbek and Turkmen) 11%, 30 minor languages (primarily Balochi and Pashai) 4%, much bilingualism

Literacy: *definition:* age 15 and over can read and write

total population: 31.5%

male: 47.2%

female: 15% (1999 est.)

Afghanistan   **Government**

Country name: *conventional long form:* Islamic State of Afghanistan; note - the self-proclaimed Taliban government refers to the country as Islamic Emirate of Afghanistan

conventional short form: Afghanistan

local long form: Dowlat-e Eslami-ye Afghanestan

local short form: Afghanestan

former: Republic of Afghanistan

Government type: no functioning central government, administered by factions

Capital: Kabul

Administrative divisions: 30 provinces (velayat, singular - velayat); Badakhshan, Badghis, Baghlan, Balkh, Bamian, Farah, Faryab, Ghazni, Ghowr, Helmand, Herat, Jowzjan, Kabol, Kandahar, Kapisa, Konar, Kondoz, Laghman, Lowgar, Nangarhar, Nimruz, Oruzgan, Paktia, Paktika, Parvan, Samangan, Sar-e Pol, Takhar, Vardak, Zabol; note - there may be two new provinces of Nurestan (Nuristan) and Khowst

Independence: 19 August 1919 (from UK control over Afghan foreign affairs)

213

National Independence Day, 19 August (1919)
holiday:

Constitution: none

Legal system: a new legal system has not been adopted but all factions tacitly agree they will follow Shari'a (Islamic law)

Suffrage: NA; previously males 15-50 years of age

Executive on 27 September 1996, the ruling members of
branch: the Afghan Government were displaced by members of the Islamic Taliban movement; the Islamic State of Afghanistan has no functioning government at this time, and the country remains divided among fighting factions

note: the Taliban have declared themselves the legitimate government of Afghanistan; however, the UN still recognizes the government of Burhanuddin RABBANI; the Organization of the Islamic Conference has left the Afghan seat vacant until the question of legitimacy can be resolved through negotiations among the warring factions; the country is essentially divided along ethnic lines; the Taliban controls the capital of Kabul and approximately two-thirds of the country including the predominately ethnic Pashtun areas in southern Afghanistan; opposing factions have their stronghold in the ethnically diverse north

Legislative non-functioning as of June 1993
branch:

Judicial branch: upper courts were non-functioning as of March 1995 (local Shari'a or Islamic law courts are functioning throughout the country)

Political parties Taliban (Religious Students Movement) **and leaders:** [Mullah Mohammad OMAR]; United National Islamic Front for the Salvation of Afghanistan or UNIFSA [Burhanuddin RABBANI, chairman; Gen. Abdul Rashid DOSTAM, vice chairman; Ahmad Shah MASOOD, military commander; Mohammed Yunis QANUNI, spokesman]; note - made up of 13 parties opposed to the Taliban including Harakat-i-Islami Afghanistan (Islamic Movement of Afghanistan), Hizb-i-Islami (Islamic Party), Hizb-i-Wahdat-i-Islami (Islamic Unity Party), Jumaat-i-Islami Afghanistan (Islamic Afghan Society), Jumbish-i-Milli (National Front), Mahaz-i-Milli-i-Islami (National Islamic Front)

Political Afghan refugees in Pakistan, Australia, US, and **pressure groups** elsewhere have organized politically; Mellat **and leaders:** (Social Democratic Party) [leader NA]; Peshawar, Pakistan-based groups such as the Coordination Council for National Unity and Understanding in Afghanistan or CUNUA [Ishaq GAILANI]; tribal elders represent traditional Pashtun leadership; Writers Union of

Free Afghanistan or WUFA [A. Rasul AMIN]

International organization participation: AsDB, CP, ECO, ESCAP, FAO, G-77, IAEA, IBRD, ICAO, ICRM, IDA, IDB, IFAD, IFC, IFRCS, ILO, IMF, Intelsat, IOC, IOM (observer), ITU, NAM, OIC, OPCW, UN, UNCTAD, UNESCO, UNIDO, UPU, WFTU, WHO, WMO, WToO

Diplomatic representation in the US: none; note - embassy operations suspended 21 August 1997

consulate(s) general: New York

Diplomatic representation from the US: the US embassy in Kabul has been closed since January 1989 due to security concerns

Flag description: three equal horizontal bands of green (top), white, and black with a gold emblem centered on the three bands; the emblem features a temple-like structure with Islamic inscriptions above and below, encircled by a wreath on the left and right and by a bolder Islamic inscription above, all of which are encircled by two crossed scimitars

note: the Taliban uses a plain white flag

Afghanistan   **Economy**

Economy - overview: Afghanistan is an extremely poor, landlocked country, highly dependent on farming and livestock raising (sheep and goats). Economic considerations have played second fiddle to political and military upheavals during two decades of war, including the nearly 10-year Soviet military occupation (which ended 15 February 1989). During that conflict one-third of the population fled the country, with Pakistan and Iran sheltering a combined peak of more than 6 million refugees. In early 2000, 2 million Afghan refugees remained in Pakistan and about 1.4 million in Iran. Gross domestic product has fallen substantially over the past 20 years because of the loss of labor and capital and the disruption of trade and transport; severe drought added to the nation's difficulties in 1998-2000. The majority of the population continues to suffer from insufficient food, clothing, housing, and medical care. Inflation remains a serious problem throughout the country. International aid can deal with only a fraction of the humanitarian problem, let alone promote economic development. In 1999-2000, internal civil strife continued, hampering both domestic economic policies and international aid efforts. Numerical data are likely to be either unavailable or unreliable. Afghanistan was by far the largest producer of opium poppies in 2000, and narcotics trafficking is a major source of revenue.

GDP: purchasing power parity - $21 billion (2000 est.)

GDP - real growth rate: NA%

GDP - per capita: purchasing power parity - $800 (2000 est.)

GDP - composition by sector: *agriculture:* 53%

industry: 28.5%

services: 18.5% (1990)

Population below poverty line: NA%

Household income or consumption by percentage share: *lowest 10%:* NA%

highest 10%: NA%

Inflation rate (consumer prices): NA%

Labor force: 10 million (2000 est.)

Labor force - by agriculture 70%, industry 15%, services 15%

occupation: (1990 est.)

Unemployment rate: NA%

Budget: *revenues:* $NA

expenditures: $NA, including capital expenditures of $NA

Industries: small-scale production of textiles, soap, furniture, shoes, fertilizer, and cement; handwoven carpets; natural gas, oil, coal, copper

Electricity - production: 420 million kWh (1999)

Electricity - production by source: *fossil fuel:* 35.71%

hydro: 64.29%

nuclear: 0%

other: 0% (1999)

Electricity - consumption: 480.6 million kWh (1999)

Electricity - 0 kWh (1999)
exports:

Electricity - 90 million kWh (1999)
imports:

Agriculture - opium poppies, wheat, fruits, nuts; wool,
  products: mutton, karakul pelts

Exports: $80 million (does not include opium) (1996
est.)

Exports - opium, fruits and nuts, handwoven carpets,
commodities: wool, cotton, hides and pelts, precious and
semi-precious gems

Exports - FSU, Pakistan, Iran, Germany, India, UK,
partners: Belgium, Luxembourg, Czech Republic

Imports: $150 million (1996 est.)

Imports - capital goods, food and petroleum products;
commodities: most consumer goods

Imports - FSU, Pakistan, Iran, Japan, Singapore, India,
partners: South Korea, Germany

Debt - external: $5.5 billion (1996 est.)

Economic aid - recipient: US provided about $70 million in humanitarian assistance in 1997; US continues to contribute to multilateral assistance through the UN programs of food aid, immunization, land mine removal, and a wide range of aid to refugees and displaced persons

Currency: afghani (AFA)

Currency code: AFA

Exchange rates: afghanis per US dollar - 4,700 (January 2000), 4,750 (February 1999), 17,000 (December 1996), 7,000 (January 1995), 1,900 (January 1994), 1,019 (March 1993), 850 (1991); note - these rates reflect the free market exchange rates rather than the official exchange rate, which was fixed at 50.600 afghanis to the dollar until 1996, when it rose to 2,262.65 per dollar, and finally became fixed again at 3,000.00 per dollar in April 1996

Fiscal year: 21 March - 20 March

Afghanistan   **Communications**

Telephones - 29,000 (1996)
main lines in
      use: *note:* there were 21,000 main lines in service
in Kabul in 1998

Telephones - NA
mobile cellular:

Telephone *general assessment:* very limited telephone and
system: telegraph service

domestic: in 1997, telecommunications links
were established between Mazar-e Sharif, Herat,
Kandahar, Jalalabad, and Kabul through satellite
and microwave systems

international: satellite earth stations - 1 Intelsat
(Indian Ocean) linked only to Iran and 1
Intersputnik (Atlantic Ocean region);
commercial satellite telephone center in Ghazni

Radio broadcast AM 7 (6 are inactive; the active station is in
stations: Kabul), FM 1, shortwave 1 (broadcasts in
Pushtu, Dari, Urdu, and English) (1999)

Radios: 167,000 (1999)

Television at least 10 (one government run central
broadcast television station in Kabul and regional stations
stations: in nine of the 30 provinces; the regional stations
operate on a reduced schedule; also, in 1997,
there was a station in Mazar-e Sharif reaching

four northern Afghanistan provinces) (1998)

Televisions: 100,000 (1999)

Internet country code: .af

Internet Service Providers (ISPs): 1 (2000)

Internet users: NA

Afghanistan   **Transportation**

Railways: *total:* 24.6 km

broad gauge: 9.6 km 1.524-m gauge from Gushgy (Turkmenistan) to Towraghondi; 15 km 1.524-m gauge from Termiz (Uzbekistan) to Kheyrabad transshipment point on south bank of Amu Darya

Highways: *total:* 21,000 km

paved: 2,793 km

unpaved: 18,207 km (1998 est.)

Waterways: 1,200 km

> *note:* chiefly Amu Darya, which handles vessels with DWT up to about 500 (2001)

Pipelines: petroleum products - Uzbekistan to Bagram and Turkmenistan to Shindand; natural gas 180 km

Ports and harbors: Kheyrabad, Shir Khan

Airports: 45 (2000 est.)

Airports - with paved runways:
total: 10

over 3,047 m: 3

2,438 to 3,047 m: 4

1,524 to 2,437 m: 2

under 914 m: 1 (2000 est.)

Airports - with unpaved runways:
total: 35

2,438 to 3,047 m: 4

1,524 to 2,437 m: 15

914 to 1,523 m: 4

under 914 m: 12 (2000 est.)

Heliports: 3 (2000 est.)

Afghanistan   **Military**

Military branches: NA; note - the military does not exist on a national basis; some elements of the former Army, Air and Air Defense Forces, National Guard, Border Guard Forces, National Police Force (Sarandoi), and tribal militias still exist but are factionalized among the various groups

Military manpower - military age: 22 years of age

Military manpower - availability: *males age 15-49:* 6,645,023 (2001 est.)

Military manpower - fit for military service: *males age 15-49:* 3,561,957 (2001 est.)

Military manpower - reaching *males:* 252,869 (2001 est.)

military age annually:	
Military expenditures - dollar figure:	$NA
Military expenditures - percent of GDP:	NA%

Afghanistan   **Transnational Issues**

Disputes - international:	support to Islamic militants worldwide by some factions; question over which group should hold Afghanistan's seat at the UN
Illicit drugs:	world's largest illicit opium producer, surpassing Burma (potential production in 1999 - 1,670 metric tons; cultivation in 1999 - 51,500 hectares, a 23% increase over 1998); a major source of hashish; increasing number of heroin-processing laboratories being set up in the country; major political factions in the country profit from drug trade